Celebrity

Classics

A unique collection of
favourite recipes from
the Carnation Kitchens

Published by: Nestlé Enterprises Limited
1185 Eglinton Avenue East
Don Mills, Ontario M3C 3C7

Printed in Canada.   ISBN 0-921392-00-1

Acknowledgements

The Multiple Sclerosis Society of Canada wishes to extend its heartfelt thanks to the many people who have made this recipe collection possible.

We offer special thanks to Carnation Canada – dedicated people whose generosity, creativity and commitment has resulted in this excellent opportunity for the Multiple Sclerosis Society of Canada to raise needed funds.

To the well-known Canadians you will meet throughout this book, we also say thank you for adding a special kind of enjoyment to the many fine recipes presented.

And finally, to all of those who worked behind the scenes to make this book a reality, we wish to express our sincere appreciation for a job well done.

The Multiple Sclerosis Society of Canada.

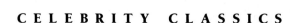

Dear Homemaker

Welcome to *Celebrity Classics* – a unique collection of all-time favourite recipes specially selected from the Carnation Kitchens with the help of an exceptional group of Canadian celebrities.

Recognized for their own unique talents and accomplishments, the fourteen celebrities in this book have two things in common:

First, they appreciate good food, carefully prepared and graciously served, at home with family or friends. That's why they are happy to be a part of *Celebrity Classics*.

Second, the group also shares a sincere and active interest in supporting the Multiple Sclerosis Society of Canada.

Multiple sclerosis is the most common neurological disease affecting young Canadian adults. Striking people between the ages of 20 to 40, multiple sclerosis attacks the myelin covering of the central nervous system. Resulting symptoms may include double vision, extreme weakness, lack of coordination, tremor and even paralysis.

Founded in 1948, the Multiple Sclerosis Society of Canada is a world leader in supporting medical research into the cause, prevention and cure of MS.

It is for this reason that the MS Society, with the co-operation of Carnation Canada, is proud to present this collection of classic recipes for your enjoyment.

All profits from the sale of this book will go to the MS Society to speed the research necessary to bring an end to this crippling disease.

On behalf of the Multiple Sclerosis Society of Canada I would like to extend my personal thanks for your support.

BON APPETIT!

Catherine McKinnon

CATHERINE McKINNON
Honorary Vice-President
National Board of Directors
MULTIPLE SCLEROSIS SOCIETY OF CANADA

C E L E B R I T Y   C L A S S I C S

Table of Contents

CELEBRITY CLASSICS

Table of Contents *cont'd*

CELEBRITY CLASSICS

Table of Contents *cont'd*

The Ⓜ symbol following some of the recipes listed indicates that the recipe can also be prepared in a microwave oven. All microwave recipes were tested in a 700 watt microwave oven.

CELEBRITY CLASSICS

A delicious beginning...

Appetizers

"Nothing gets the party, the dinner or any friendly gathering off to a fast start like the welcoming taste of delicious appetizers. Be sure to try the dishes on these next few pages. They're extra special crowd pleasers."

CATHERINE McKINNON

A native Maritimer, Catherine McKinnon first came to national prominence on Singalong Jubilee and on Don Messer's Jubilee. Miss McKinnon has also appeared in numerous television specials, hosted her own TV shows and currently stars on stage in both musical comedies and in serious dramatic roles. Catherine is National Spokesperson for the Multiple Sclerosis Society of Canada.

Spinach-Bacon Mini Quiches

	Sufficient pastry for 9-inch (23 cm) double crust pie	
1	pkg (300 g) frozen chopped spinach, thawed, squeezed dry	1
1 cup	shredded Swiss cheese	250 mL
6	slices crisp crumbled bacon	6
¼ cup	chopped onion	50 mL
¾ cup	CARNATION Instant Skim Milk Powder *plus* water to make 1½ cups (375 mL)	175 mL
3	eggs	3
3 Tbsp	flour	45 mL
2 Tbsp	butter, melted	30 mL
1 tsp	salt	5 mL
1 Tbsp	grated Parmesan cheese	15 mL

Roll out pastry; cut into twelve (5-inch/12 cm) circles. Set each circle loosely into a large 3-inch (7 cm) muffin cup; chill. Toss together spinach, Swiss cheese, bacon and onion; spoon into pastry shells. Place skim milk powder plus water, eggs, flour, butter and salt in blender container. Cover and blend until smooth. Pour over cheese mixture in shells; sprinkle with Parmesan cheese. Bake in 375°F (190°C) oven 30 to 35 min. or until set.

Makes 1 dozen.

Party Cheese Mold

2	envelopes unflavoured gelatin	2
1 cup	cold water	250 mL
1 tsp	chicken bouillon mix	5 mL
1	pkg (250 g) cream cheese, softened	1
1 cup	process cheese spread	250 mL
2 Tbsp	minced onion	30 mL
¼ cup	finely-chopped pecans	50 mL
3	slices crisp crumbled bacon	3
	Dash hot pepper sauce	
⅔ cup	*undiluted* CARNATION 2% Evaporated Milk	150 mL
1 Tbsp	lemon juice	15 mL
	Assorted crackers	

Sprinkle gelatin over water in small saucepan. Let stand 10 min. to soften. Stir in chicken bouillon mix. Cook and stir over low heat until gelatin is dissolved; cool. Beat together cream cheese and process cheese until smooth. Slowly add dissolved gelatin mixture; beat until thoroughly blended. Stir in onion, pecans, bacon and hot pepper sauce. Chill until consistency of unbeaten egg whites; stir occasionally. Pour evaporated milk into metal cake pan. Chill in freezer until soft ice crystals form around edges of pan, about 10-15 min. Whip in small mixer bowl until stiff, about 1 min. Add lemon juice. Whip very stiff, about 1-2 min. longer. Fold into cheese mixture. Pour into 5-cup (1.25 L) shallow mold. Chill until firm. Unmold and serve with assorted crackers.

Makes about 5 cups (1.25 L).

Scallops Duchesse

5 Tbsp	butter, divided	75 mL
4 cups	sliced fresh mushrooms	1000 mL
1 lb	frozen scallops, thawed	500 g
½ cup	water	125 mL
¾ tsp	salt	3 mL
¼ tsp	dried thyme leaves, crushed	1 mL
1	bay leaf	1
3 Tbsp	flour	45 mL
1½ cups	*undiluted* CARNATION Evaporated Milk	375 mL
1 cup	shredded 'old' Cheddar cheese	250 mL
	Buttered Bread Crumbs	

Melt 2 Tbsp (30 mL) of the butter in medium saucepan. Sauté mushrooms until tender and any liquid has evaporated. Cut scallops in half; add to mushrooms with water, salt, thyme and bay leaf. Bring to boil. Cover and simmer 3 to 4 min. or until cooked. Drain; reserve 1 cup (250 mL) broth. Discard bay leaf. Melt remaining 3 Tbsp (45 mL) butter in saucepan. Blend in flour. Gradually stir in evaporated milk and reserved broth. Cook and stir over medium heat until mixture comes to a boil and thickens. Add cheese; stir until melted. Add mushrooms and scallops. Spoon into 6 individual shallow baking dishes. Top with Buttered Bread Crumbs. Bake in 350°F (180°C) oven 25 to 30 min. or until hot and bubbly.

Buttered Bread Crumbs: Combine ¾ cup (175 mL) fine, dry bread crumbs and 2 Tbsp (30 mL) melted butter; toss well.

Makes 6 servings.

Honey Garlic Meatballs

2 lbs	lean ground beef	1 kg
1	can (10 ozs/284 mL) water chestnuts, drained, chopped	1
1 cup	fine dry bread crumbs	250 mL
¾ cup	*undiluted* CARNATION Evaporated Milk	175 mL
½ cup	finely-chopped onion	125 mL
2	eggs	2
2 tsp	salt	10 mL
1 Tbsp	butter	15 mL
4	cloves garlic, crushed, chopped	4
¾ cup	ketchup	175 mL
½ cup	liquid honey	125 mL
¼ cup	soy sauce	50 mL

Combine beef, water chestnuts, bread crumbs, evaporated milk, onion, eggs and salt; mix well. Shape mixture into 1-inch (2.5 cm) balls. Place in single layer in 15 x 10 x ¾-inch (2 L) jelly roll pan. Bake in 500°F (260°C) oven 10 to 12 min. or until browned. Drain. Melt butter in large saucepan; sauté garlic until tender. Add ketchup, honey and soy sauce. Bring to boil. Reduce heat; cover and simmer 5 min. Add meatballs to sauce. Simmer, uncovered, 5 to 10 min.; stir occasionally.

To Microwave: Prepare meatballs as above. Arrange 25 meatballs at a time in 10-inch (25 cm) glass pie plate. Microwave, uncovered, at HIGH (100%) 5 to 6 min. or until cooked. Repeat with remaining meatballs. Place butter and garlic in 3-quart (3 L) glass bowl. Microwave, uncovered, at HIGH (100%) 1½ min. or until garlic is cooked. Stir in ketchup, honey and soy sauce. Microwave, uncovered, at HIGH (100%) 4 min.; stir once while cooking. Add meatballs to sauce. Microwave, covered, at MEDIUM (50%) 5 min. or until hot; stir twice while cooking.

Makes about 100 meatballs.

APPETIZERS

Creamy Mushroom Appetizers

¼ cup	butter	50 mL
2½ cups	finely-chopped mushrooms	625 mL
¼ cup	finely-chopped green onions	50 mL
2 Tbsp	flour	30 mL
1 cup	*undiluted* CARNATION 2% Evaporated Milk	250 mL
2 Tbsp	finely-chopped parsley	30 mL
½ tsp	lemon juice	2 mL
	Salt and pepper	
	Toast Cups	

Melt butter in medium saucepan; sauté mushrooms and onions until tender and any liquid has evaporated. Blend in flour. Gradually stir in evaporated milk. Cook and stir over medium heat until mixture comes to a boil and thickens. Remove from heat. Stir in parsley and lemon juice. Add salt and pepper to taste. Cover and chill until serving time. Divide mixture evenly among Toast Cups. Bake in 350°F (180°C) oven 15 to 20 min. or until hot. Garnish.

Toast Cups: Butter 48 (2-inch/5 cm) muffin cups. Slightly flatten 48 bread slices. Cut a 3-inch (7 cm) round from each bread slice. Press bread rounds into muffin cups. Brush lightly with ¼ cup (50 mL) melted butter. Bake in 400°F (200°C) oven 12 min. or until lightly browned. Cool.

Makes 48 appetizers.

Appetizer
Cheese Squares

1½ cups	cheese flavoured cracker crumbs	375 mL
¼ cup	butter, melted	50 mL
1	pkg (250 g) cream cheese, softened	1
2	eggs	2
1 Tbsp	flour	15 mL
⅔ cup	*undiluted* CARNATION Evaporated Milk	150 mL
1 tsp	lemon juice	5 mL
½ tsp	Worcestershire sauce	2 mL
6 drops	hot pepper sauce	6
½ cup	chopped green onions	125 mL
¼ cup	chopped pimento	50 mL

Combine cracker crumbs and butter. Press onto bottom of 9-inch (23 cm) square baking pan. Bake in 350°F (180°C) oven 5 min. Place cream cheese, eggs, flour, evaporated milk, lemon juice, Worcestershire and hot pepper sauces in blender container. Cover and blend until smooth. Sprinkle onions and pimento over crust. Carefully pour cream cheese mixture over all. Bake in 350°F (180°C) oven 25 to 30 min. or until knife inserted near centre comes out clean. Cool slightly; cut into bite-size squares. Serve warm or chilled.

Makes 1 pan.

Nachos

1 Tbsp	butter	15 mL
1 Tbsp	flour	15 mL
1 tsp	taco seasoning mix	5 mL
⅔ cup	*undiluted* CARNATION 2% Evaporated Milk	150 mL
⅓ cup	water	75 mL
1 cup	shredded Cheddar cheese	250 mL
	Tortilla chips	
	Bottled chili salsa	

Melt butter in medium saucepan. Blend in flour and taco seasoning. Gradually stir in evaporated milk and water. Cook and stir over medium heat until mixture comes to a boil and thickens. Remove from heat. Add cheese; stir until melted. Pour sauce over tortilla chips; serve with chili salsa for dipping.

To Microwave: Place butter in 1-quart (1 L) glass measure. Microwave, uncovered, at HIGH (100%) 30 sec. Blend in flour and taco seasoning. Gradually stir in evaporated milk and water. Microwave, uncovered, at HIGH (100%) 3 to 4 min. or until sauce boils and thickens; stir 3 times while cooking. Add cheese; stir until melted. Complete as above.

Makes about 1⅓ cups (325 mL) sauce.

A P P E T I Z E R S

Nice 'n' Nippy Cheddar Spread

½ cup	*undiluted* CARNATION 2% Evaporated Milk	125 mL
1	pkg (250 g) cream cheese, softened	1
1 tsp	Worcestershire sauce	5 mL
1½ cups	shredded 'old' Cheddar cheese	375 mL
	Seasoned salt	
	Assorted crackers	

Combine evaporated milk, cream cheese and Worcestershire sauce in blender container. Cover and blend on high speed until smooth. Add Cheddar cheese, part at a time, blending until smooth. Scrape down sides of container if necessary. Add seasoned salt to taste. Cover and chill at least 1 hour to blend flavours. Serve with assorted crackers.

Makes about 1⅔ cups (400 mL).

Curried Egg Spread

⅓ cup	CARNATION Instant Skim Milk Powder	75 mL
¼ cup	mayonnaise *or* salad dressing	50 mL
4	hard-cooked eggs, finely chopped	4
2 Tbsp	finely-chopped green onions	30 mL
2 Tbsp	finely-chopped celery	30 mL
	Pinch curry powder	
	Salt and pepper	
	Assorted crackers	

Combine skim milk powder, mayonnaise, eggs, onions, celery and curry powder; mix thoroughly. Add salt and pepper to taste. Chill at least 1 hour to blend flavours. Serve with assorted crackers.

Makes about 1½ cups (375 mL).

APPETIZERS

Creamy, rich and tasty...

Soups

"*Nothing beats the warmly satisfying taste of a homemade soup, especially on a cold Canadian winter's day.*

Here are a few of my very favourites – chowders and hearty vegetable varieties to please family and guests alike."

BARBARA HAMILTON

One of Canada's best loved comedic actresses, Barbara Hamilton has entertained us on television, in movies and on stage for many years. Miss Hamilton may be best known as the star of Canada's much-acclaimed and longest running satirical review, Spring Thaw and for her award winning portrayal of Marilla in Anne of Green Gables.

Springtime
Potato 'n' Leek Soup

2 Tbsp	butter	30 mL
½ cup	sliced leeks *or* onion	125 mL
2 cups	thinly-sliced peeled potatoes	500 mL
2⅔ cups	water, divided	650 mL
1 Tbsp	chicken bouillon mix	15 mL
1 cup	CARNATION Instant Skim Milk Powder	250 mL
	Salt and pepper	

Melt butter in medium saucepan. Sauté leeks until tender. Add potatoes, 1⅔ cups (400 mL) of the water and bouillon mix. Bring to boil. Cover and simmer 15 min. or until potatoes are tender. Spoon mixture into blender container; cover and blend until smooth. Add remaining 1 cup (250 mL) water and skim milk powder to blender container. Cover and blend until smoothly combined. Add salt and pepper to taste. Return to saucepan and reheat to serving temperature if necessary. Garnish.

Makes about 4 cups (1 L).

Creamy Clam Chowder

3	slices bacon, chopped	3
½ cup	chopped onion	125 mL
1	can (5.2 ozs/147 g) baby clams, undrained	1
	Water	
1 cup	diced peeled potatoes	250 mL
¼ tsp	celery salt	1 mL
1	can (385 mL) CARNATION Evaporated Milk	1
2 Tbsp	flour	30 mL
	Salt and pepper	

Cook bacon until crisp in large saucepan. Drain, reserving drippings; set bacon aside. Sauté onion in reserved drippings until tender. Drain clams, reserving liquid; set clams aside. Add water to clam liquid to make 1¾ cups (425 mL); stir into onion mixture. Add potatoes and celery salt. Bring to boil. Cover and simmer 15 min. or until potatoes are tender. Combine evaporated milk and flour until smooth; add to pan. Cook and stir over medium heat until mixture comes to a boil and thickens. Stir in reserved clams. Add salt and pepper to taste. Garnish with cooked bacon.

Makes about 5 cups (1.25 L).

Swiss Onion Soup
au Gratin

¼ cup	butter	50 mL
3½ cups	sliced halved onions	875 mL
3 Tbsp	flour	45 mL
3 cups	water, divided	750 mL
1 Tbsp	chicken bouillon mix	15 mL
1 cup	shredded Swiss cheese, divided	225 mL
1 cup	CARNATION Instant Skim Milk Powder	250 mL
	Salt and pepper	
1 cup	seasoned croutons	250 mL

Melt butter in medium saucepan; sauté onions until tender. Blend in flour. Gradually stir in 2½ cups (625 mL) of the water and bouillon mix. Cook and stir over medium heat until mixture comes to a boil and thickens. Cover and simmer 15 min. Add ¾ cup (175 mL) of the cheese; stir until melted. Combine remaining ½ cup (125 mL) water and skim milk powder; stir into soup. Add salt and pepper to taste. Ladle into 4 oven-proof soup bowls. Sprinkle with croutons. Top with remaining ¼ cup (50 mL) cheese. Place bowls on baking sheet. Broil until cheese is melted.

Makes 4 servings.

Creamy Carrot Potage

4 cups	sliced carrots	1000 mL
1½ cups	sliced peeled potatoes	375 mL
1½ cups	sliced onions	375 mL
2½ cups	water	625 mL
2 Tbsp	butter	30 mL
4 tsp	chicken bouillon mix	20 mL
1	can (385 mL) CARNATION 2% Evaporated Milk	1
2 Tbsp	flour	30 mL
	Seasoned salt	

Combine carrots, potatoes, onions, water, butter and bouillon mix in large saucepan. Bring to boil. Cover and simmer 20 min. or until vegetables are tender. Mash vegetables coarsely with potato masher. Combine evaporated milk and flour until smooth; add to pan. Cook and stir over medium heat until mixture comes to a boil and thickens. Add seasoned salt to taste.

Makes about 7 cups (1.75 L).

Chicken
Corn Chowder

2½ lb	chicken, cut up	1.25 kg
2½ cups	water	625 mL
2 cups	chopped onions	500 mL
2 cups	diced peeled potatoes	500 mL
½ cup	sliced celery	125 mL
1 Tbsp	chicken bouillon mix	15 mL
2	cans (385 mL *each*) CARNATION 2% Evaporated Milk	2
¼ cup	all purpose flour	50 mL
1	can (14 ozs/398 mL) cream-style corn	1
	Salt and pepper	

Place chicken pieces in large saucepan or Dutch oven; add water and onions. Bring to boil. Cover and simmer 45 min. or until tender. Remove chicken from pan. Add potatoes, celery and bouillon mix; simmer 15 min. longer or until vegetables are tender. Remove bones and skin from chicken pieces; dice meat. Combine evaporated milk and flour until smooth; add to pan. Cook and stir over medium heat until mixture comes to a boil and thickens. Stir in chicken and corn. Add salt and pepper to taste. Reheat to serving temperature if necessary.

Makes about 12 cups (3 L).

SOUPS

Creamy Mushroom Soup

1	can (10 ozs/284 mL) sliced mushrooms, undrained	1
	Water	
¼ cup	chopped onion	50 mL
2 tsp	chicken bouillon mix	10 mL
¼ cup	butter	50 mL
⅓ cup	all purpose flour	75 mL
1	can (385 mL) CARNATION Evaporated Milk	1
1⅓ cups	water	325 mL
	Salt and pepper	

Drain mushrooms; add water to liquid to make 2 cups (500 mL). Place in medium saucepan; add mushrooms, onion and bouillon mix. Bring to boil. Cover and simmer 15 min. Pour into blender container. Cover and blend until mushrooms are finely chopped; set aside. Melt butter in large saucepan. Blend in flour. Gradually stir in evaporated milk and 1⅓ cups (325 mL) water. Cook and stir over medium heat until mixture comes to a boil and thickens. Stir in mushroom mixture. Add salt and pepper to taste.

To Microwave: Drain mushrooms; add water to mushroom liquid to make 2 cups (500 mL). Place in 1-quart (1 L) glass measure. Add mushrooms, onion and bouillon mix. Microwave, covered, at HIGH (100%) 7 to 10 min. or until vegetables are tender; stir twice while cooking. Pour into blender container. Cover and blend until mushrooms are finely chopped; set aside. Place butter in 2-quart (2 L) glass measure. Microwave, uncovered, at HIGH (100%) 45 sec. Blend in flour. Gradually stir in evaporated milk and water. Microwave, uncovered, at HIGH (100%) 3 to 4 min. or until mixture boils and thickens; stir 3 times while cooking. Complete as above.

Makes about 6 cups (1.5 L).

SOUPS

Cream of
Fresh Asparagus Soup

1 lb	fresh asparagus	500 g
1½ cups	water	375 mL
1 cup	chopped onion	250 mL
1 Tbsp	chicken bouillon mix	15 mL
¼ tsp	garlic salt	1 mL
1 cup	*undiluted* CARNATION 2% Evaporated Milk	250 mL
1 Tbsp	flour	15 mL
	Salt and pepper	
	Seasoned croutons	

Snap tough ends off asparagus; discard. Cut asparagus into 1-inch (2.5 cm) pieces. Place in medium saucepan. Stir in water, onion, bouillon mix and garlic salt. Bring to boil. Cover and simmer 10 to 15 min. or until asparagus is tender. Pour into blender container. Add evaporated milk and flour. Cover and blend until smooth. Return mixture to saucepan. Cook and stir over medium heat until mixture comes to a boil and thickens. Add salt and pepper to taste. Serve hot with seasoned croutons.

Makes about 4 cups (1 L).

Hearty
Split Pea Soup

2 cups	dried yellow split peas	500 mL
6 cups	water	1500 mL
1½ tsp	salt	7 mL
2 cups	chopped ham	500 mL
¾ cup	chopped carrot	175 mL
½ cup	chopped onion	125 mL
2 Tbsp	butter	30 mL
1	can (385 mL) CARNATION Evaporated Milk	1
¼ tsp	cayenne	1 mL

Combine peas, water and salt in large saucepan. Bring to boil; boil 2 min. Remove from heat; let stand 1 hour. (Do not change water.) Add ham, carrot, onion and butter to peas. Bring to boil. Cover and simmer 35 to 40 min. or until peas are tender. Stir in evaporated milk and cayenne. Reheat to serving temperature.

Makes about 8 cups (2 L).

Deliciously Fresh...

Salads

From Paquetville, Acadia, to the Olympia in Paris, Edith Butler has
travelled a long road of song that has taken her to many places around the
world. In recognition of her exceptional artistic abilities she was awarded
the Order of Canada and l'Ordre du Merite de la culture française.

Pasta Salad Milano

½ cup	*undiluted* CARNATION 2% Evaporated Milk	125 mL
¼ cup	vinegar	50 mL
1	egg*	1
½ tsp	dry mustard	2 mL
½ tsp	dried Italian seasoning	2 mL
½ tsp	sugar	2 mL
¼ tsp	salt	1 mL
1	clove garlic, crushed	1
⅔ cup	vegetable oil	150 mL
3 cups	rotini, tortellini *or* medium shell pasta	750 mL
2 cups	broccoli flowerets	500 mL
½ cup	slivered sweet red pepper	125 mL
⅓ cup	sliced green onions	75 mL
	Salt and pepper	
	Cucumber slices	

Combine evaporated milk, vinegar, egg, mustard, Italian seasoning, sugar, salt and garlic in blender container; cover and blend on high speed until smooth. With motor running, gradually add oil in thin stream. Continue blending until slightly thickened and smooth. Chill 1 hour to blend flavours. Cook pasta according to package directions; drain; cool. Cook broccoli in boiling salted water until crisp-tender; drain; cool. Combine cooked pasta, broccoli, red pepper, onions and dressing; toss lightly to combine. Add salt and pepper to taste. Chill 1 hour to blend flavours. Garnish individual servings with cucumber slices.

Makes about 6 cups (1.5 L).

*Use clean uncracked egg.

S A L A D S

Summertime Potato Salad

6 cups	diced peeled cooked potatoes	1500 mL
½ cup	*undiluted* CARNATION Evaporated Milk	125 mL
2	hard-cooked eggs, chopped	2
1 cup	thinly-sliced celery	250 mL
½ cup	thinly-sliced radishes	125 mL
½ cup	thinly-sliced green onions	125 mL
1 cup	mayonnaise *or* salad dressing	250 mL
2 Tbsp	vinegar	30 mL
1 tsp	dried dill weed	5 mL
	Salt and pepper	

Place potatoes in large bowl. Pour evaporated milk over potatoes. Add eggs, celery, radishes and green onions; toss lightly. Combine mayonnaise, vinegar and dill weed. Pour over potato mixture. Toss until thoroughly combined. Add salt and pepper to taste. Chill at least 1 hour to blend flavours.

Makes 10 to 12 servings.

Spinach Salad
Deluxe

8	slices bacon, chopped	8
3 Tbsp	cider vinegar	45 mL
¼ tsp	sugar	1 mL
	Pinch dry mustard	
½ cup	*undiluted* CARNATION 2% Evaporated Milk	125 mL
½ cup	mayonnaise *or* salad dressing	125 mL
	Salt and pepper	
8 cups	washed drained torn spinach	2 L
4	hard-cooked eggs, sliced	4
1½ cups	sliced fresh mushrooms	375 mL

Cook bacon until crisp in medium saucepan. Drain, reserving 2 Tbsp (30 mL) drippings; set bacon aside. Stir vinegar, sugar and dry mustard into reserved drippings. Gradually stir in evaporated milk. Blend in mayonnaise. Add salt and pepper to taste. Cover and chill at least 1 hour to blend flavours. To serve, toss together spinach, eggs, mushrooms and reserved bacon in large salad bowl. Pour dressing over individual servings.

To Microwave: Place bacon in 1½-quart (1.5 L) shallow glass casserole. Microwave, loosely covered, at HIGH (100%) 8 to 9 min. or until crisp; stir twice while cooking. Set bacon aside; reserve 2 Tbsp (30 mL) drippings. Stir vinegar, sugar and dry mustard into reserved drippings. Gradually stir in evaporated milk. Blend in mayonnaise. Add salt and pepper to taste. Complete as above.

Makes 6 servings.

S A L A D S

Salmon Salad Mousse

2	envelopes unflavoured gelatin	2
1⅓ cups	cold water	325 mL
2 tsp	chicken bouillon mix	10 mL
4 Tbsp	lemon juice, divided	60 mL
1	can (15.5 ozs/439 g) salmon, drained, flaked	1
½ cup	finely-chopped celery	125 mL
½ cup	peeled seeded chopped cucumber	125 mL
½ cup	mayonnaise *or* salad dressing	125 mL
½ tsp	dry mustard	2 mL
½ tsp	salt	2 mL
⅔ cup	*undiluted* CARNATION 2% Evaporated Milk	150 mL

Sprinkle gelatin over water in saucepan. Let stand 10 min. to soften. Stir in bouillon mix. Cook and stir over low heat until gelatin dissolves; cool. Stir in 2 Tbsp (30 mL) of the lemon juice, salmon, celery, cucumber, mayonnaise, dry mustard and salt. Chill until consistency of unbeaten egg whites; stir occasionally. Pour evaporated milk into metal cake pan. Chill in freezer until soft ice crystals form around edges of pan (10-15 min.). Whip in small mixer bowl until stiff (about 1 min.). Add remaining 2 Tbsp (30 mL) lemon juice. Whip very stiff (about 1-2 min. longer). Fold into gelatin mixture. Pour into 7-cup (1.75 L) mold. Chill until firm. Unmold to serve.

Makes about 7 cups (1.75 L).

Chicken Wild Rice Salad

1	pkg (170 g) long grain and wild rice mix	1
1 Tbsp	chicken bouillon mix	15 mL
2 cups	diced cooked chicken	500 mL
1 cup	diced green pepper	250 mL
½ cup	shredded carrot	125 mL
⅓ cup	thinly-sliced green onions	75 mL
3 Tbsp	lemon juice	45 mL
1 cup	*undiluted* CARNATION Evaporated Milk	250 mL
¾ cup	mayonnaise *or* salad dressing	175 mL
	Salt and pepper	

Cook rice according to package directions. Stir in bouillon mix; cool. Add chicken, green pepper, carrot and onions to rice; toss lightly to combine. Stir lemon juice into evaporated milk. Blend in mayonnaise. Add salt and pepper to taste. Pour over rice mixture; stir until well combined. Chill at least 1 hour to blend flavours.

Makes about 6 cups (1.5 L).

Frozen Fruit Salad Squares

1 cup	marshmallow cream	250 mL
1 cup	strawberry yogurt	250 mL
1	pkg (425 g) frozen sweetened sliced strawberries, thawed, undrained	1
1 cup	*undiluted* CARNATION Evaporated Milk	250 mL
2 Tbsp	lemon juice	30 mL
1	can (14 ozs/398 mL) crushed pineapple, drained	1
1	medium banana, thinly sliced	1
½ cup	chopped nuts	125 mL

Combine marshmallow cream and yogurt in large mixing bowl. Let stand about 30 min.; stir occasionally. Stir in undrained strawberries. Pour evaporated milk into metal cake pan. Chill in freezer until soft ice crystals form around edges of pan (10-15 min.). Whip in small mixer bowl until stiff (about 1 min.). Add lemon juice. Whip very stiff (about 1-2 min. longer). Fold into marshmallow-yogurt mixture. Fold in drained pineapple, banana and nuts. Spoon mixture into shallow 2-quart (2 L) rectangular baking dish. Cover and freeze until firm. Let stand at room temperature about 5 min. before cutting into squares. Garnish.

Makes 8 to 10 servings.

The Italian classic...

Pasta

"I've always known pasta is a long distance swimmer's best friend. There are so many mouth-watering ways to prepare this great energy builder. Here are just a few of my favourites."

JOCELYN MUIR

Jocelyn Muir is a world class marathon swimmer who, in the "Summer of '87", swam the 522.5 mile circumference of Lake Ontario for the Multiple Sclerosis Society. Miss Muir's other accomplishments include the 1982 Women's World Marathon Swim Championship. She was also, at the age of 15, the youngest person to swim across Lake Ontario.

Linguine
with Clam Sauce

1	can (5 ozs/142 g) baby clams, undrained	1
	Water	
6 Tbsp	butter, divided	90 mL
¾ cup	chopped onion	175 mL
1½ cups	peeled chopped fresh tomatoes*	375 mL
¾ tsp	dried basil leaves, crushed	3 mL
	Salt and pepper	
2 Tbsp	flour	30 mL
¾ cup	*undiluted* CARNATION 2% Evaporated Milk	175 mL
½ cup	grated Parmesan cheese	125 mL
2 Tbsp	chopped parsley	30 mL
12 ozs	linguine	375 g

Drain clams, reserving liquid; set clams aside. Add water to liquid to make ¾ cup (175 mL); set liquid aside. Melt 3 Tbsp (45 mL) of the butter in saucepan. Sauté onion until tender. Add tomatoes and basil. Bring to boil. Cover and simmer 15 min.; stir occasionally. Add clams. Add salt and pepper to taste; keep warm. Melt remaining 3 Tbsp (45 mL) butter in another saucepan. Blend in flour. Gradually stir in evaporated milk and reserved clam-water mixture. Cook and stir over medium heat until mixture comes to a boil and thickens. Remove from heat. Add cheese and parsley; stir until well combined. Cover sauce; keep warm. Cook linguine according to package directions; drain. To serve, top linguine with cheese sauce and clam sauce. Serve immediately.

Makes 4 servings.

*Or 1 can (14 ozs/398 mL) tomatoes, drained and chopped.

Macaroni and Cheese Italiano

1½ cups	elbow macaroni	375 mL
2 Tbsp	butter	30 mL
3 Tbsp	finely-chopped onion	45 mL
2 Tbsp	flour	30 mL
¾ tsp	dried oregano leaves, crushed	4 mL
1	can (385 mL) CARNATION 2% Evaporated Milk	1
¾ cup	water	175 mL
1½ cups	grated Parmesan cheese	375 mL
	Salt and pepper	
1	can (28 ozs/796 mL) tomatoes, drained, coarsely chopped	1
	Buttered Bread Crumbs	

Cook macaroni according to package directions; drain. Melt butter in large saucepan. Add onion; sauté until tender. Blend in flour and oregano. Gradually stir in evaporated milk and water. Cook and stir over medium heat until mixture comes to a boil and thickens. Stir in cheese until well combined. Add salt and pepper to taste. Combine macaroni and sauce. Spoon half the chopped tomato in bottom of 2-quart (2 L) casserole; top with half the macaroni mixture. Repeat layers. Top with Buttered Bread Crumbs. Bake, uncovered, in 350°F (180°C) oven 25 to 30 min. or until browned and bubbly.

Buttered Bread Crumbs: Toss 1½ cups (375 mL) fresh bread crumbs with 3 Tbsp (45 mL) melted butter.

Makes 4 to 6 servings.

Chicken Noodle Casserole

2 cups	wide egg noodles	500 mL
1	pkg (300 g) frozen chopped broccoli	1
¼ cup	butter	50 mL
½ cup	finely-chopped onion	125 mL
¼ cup	all purpose flour	50 mL
2 tsp	chicken bouillon mix	10 mL
¼ tsp	poultry seasoning	1 mL
1	can (385 mL) CARNATION Evaporated Milk	1
1⅓ cups	water	325 mL
¼ cup	grated Parmesan cheese	50 mL
	Salt and pepper	
3 cups	cut-up cooked chicken *or* turkey	750 mL
	Buttered Bread Crumbs	

Cook noodles and broccoli according to package directions; drain.
Melt butter in large saucepan. Sauté onion until tender. Blend in flour,
bouillon mix and poultry seasoning. Gradually stir in evaporated milk
and water. Cook and stir over medium heat until mixture comes to a
boil and thickens. Add cheese; stir until well combined. Add salt and
pepper to taste. Fold in noodles, broccoli and chicken. Turn into 2-quart
(2 L) casserole. Top with Buttered Bread Crumbs. Bake in 350°F (180°C)
oven 30 to 35 min. or until heated through.

Buttered Bread Crumbs: Toss ½ cup (125 mL) fresh bread crumbs
with 1 Tbsp (15 mL) melted butter.

Makes 4 to 5 servings.

Green and White Pasta Ribbons

3 Tbsp	butter	45 mL
2	cloves garlic, crushed, chopped	2
2 Tbsp	flour	30 mL
1½ tsp	dried basil leaves, crushed	7 mL
1 tsp	chicken bouillon mix	5 mL
1 cup	*undiluted* CARNATION 2% Evaporated Milk	250 mL
¾ cup	water	175 mL
½ cup	shredded mozzarella cheese	125 mL
¼ cup	grated Parmesan cheese	50 mL
1 cup	frozen peas, thawed	250 mL
½ cup	coarsely-chopped ham	125 mL
8 ozs	linguine (green and white mixed)	250 g
	Grated Parmesan cheese	

Melt butter in medium saucepan; sauté garlic until tender. Blend in flour, basil and bouillon mix. Gradually stir in evaporated milk and water. Cook and stir over medium heat until mixture comes to a boil and thickens. Add mozzarella and Parmesan cheeses; stir until well combined. Stir in peas and ham. Cover sauce; keep warm. Cook linguine according to package directions; drain. Pour sauce over linguine; toss well. Serve with more Parmesan cheese if desired.

Makes 4 servings.

Quick 'n' Easy
Skillet Supper

2 cups	uncooked medium noodles	500 mL
¾ lb	cooked ham	375 g
2 Tbsp	butter	30 mL
1 cup	sliced onion	250 mL
½ cup	diced green pepper	125 mL
1	can (10 ozs/284 mL) sliced mushrooms, undrained	1
1	can (10 ozs/284 mL) cream of mushroom soup	1
⅔ cup	*undiluted* CARNATION Evaporated Milk	150 mL
1 tsp	prepared mustard	5 mL

Cook noodles according to package directions; drain. Slice ham into strips. Melt butter in large frypan. Sauté ham, onion and green pepper until tender. Drain mushrooms, reserving ¼ cup (50 mL) liquid. Add mushrooms and reserved liquid, soup, evaporated milk and mustard to pan; stir well. Bring to boil. Cover and simmer 10 min. Add noodles; mix well. Reheat to serving temperature; stir occasionally.

To Microwave: Prepare noodles and ham as above. Combine ham, butter, onion and green pepper in 2-quart (2 L) shallow glass baking dish. Microwave, uncovered, at HIGH (100%) 9 to 10 min. or until vegetables are tender; stir three times while cooking. Combine all ingredients as above. Microwave, covered, at HIGH (100%) 4 to 5 min. or until heated through; stir twice while cooking.

Makes 4 servings.

Spaghetti Carbonara

16 ozs	spaghetti	500 g
8	slices bacon, chopped	8
1 cup	*undiluted* CARNATION Evaporated Milk	250 mL
2 Tbsp	butter	30 mL
4	eggs	4
⅓ cup	grated Parmesan cheese	75 mL
1 Tbsp	chopped parsley	15 mL
	Salt and pepper	

Cook spaghetti according to package directions. Meanwhile, cook bacon until crisp in medium saucepan. Drain, reserving 3 Tbsp (45 mL) bacon drippings; set bacon aside. Wipe pan clean. Return reserved drippings to pan; add evaporated milk and butter. Cook and stir until butter is melted; keep warm but do not boil. Combine eggs and cheese in bowl; mix well. Drain spaghetti; place in large bowl. Add hot evaporated milk mixture, egg mixture, bacon and parsley. Toss well to coat. Add salt and pepper to taste. Serve immediately.

Makes 6 servings.

PASTA

Unique and refreshing...

Beverages

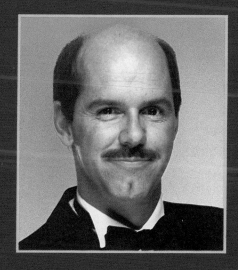

"If you're like me you find it hard to resist the smooth creamy taste of a great homemade drink. Here's a selection of some of my more unusual favourites."

JACKSON DAVIES

Jackson Davies is one of Canada's most versatile actors. Best known for his award winning role as Constable John on the CBC series "The Beachcombers," Mr. Davies has also appeared in numerous television and stage productions as well as a number of feature and made-for-TV films including "Christmas Pageant" and "Hitchhiker."

Strawberry Yogurt Frost

1	pkg (425 g) frozen sweetened sliced strawberries	1
1 cup	plain yogurt	250 mL
⅓ cup	CARNATION Instant Skim Milk Powder	75 mL
¾ cup	water	175 mL
1 tsp	vanilla	5 mL

Cut frozen block of strawberries in half. Place yogurt, skim milk powder, water, strawberries and vanilla in blender container. Cover and blend at high speed until smooth.

Makes about 4 cups (1 L).

Tropical Treat

¾ cup	chilled unsweetened pineapple juice	175 mL
1	egg*	1
⅓ cup	CARNATION Instant Skim Milk Powder	75 mL
3 Tbsp	sugar	45 mL
1 tsp	vanilla	5 mL
1	large ripe banana, sliced	1
12	ice cubes	12

Combine pineapple juice, egg, skim milk powder, sugar, vanilla, banana and ice cubes in blender container. Cover and blend at high speed until smooth.

Makes about 3 cups (750 mL).

*Use clean uncracked egg.

Bananaberry Shake

1 cup	cold milk	250 mL
1	medium ripe banana, sliced	1
1	envelope CARNATION Strawberry Instant Breakfast	1
2	ice cubes	2

Combine milk, banana, instant breakfast and ice cubes in blender container. Cover and blend at high speed until smooth.

Makes about 2½ cups (625 mL).

Chocolate Breakfast Shake

1 cup	cold milk	250 mL
1	medium ripe banana, sliced	1
1	envelope, CARNATION Chocolate Instant Breakfast	1
2	scoops chocolate ice cream	2

Combine milk, banana, instant breakfast and ice cream in blender container. Cover and blend at high speed until smooth.

Makes about 2 cups (500 mL).

BEVERAGES

Orange Cooler

¾ cup	cold water	175 mL
1	egg*	1
¾ cup	frozen orange juice concentrate	175 mL
½ cup	CARNATION Instant Skim Milk Powder	125 mL
3 Tbsp	sugar	45 mL
1 tsp	vanilla	5 mL
10	ice cubes	10

Combine water, egg, orange juice concentrate, skim milk powder, sugar, vanilla and ice cubes in blender container. Cover and blend at high speed until smooth.

Makes about 4 cups (1 L).

*Use clean uncracked egg.

Frosty Eggnog

4	eggs*	4
¼ cup	cold water	50 mL
1 cup	CARNATION Instant Skim Milk Powder	250 mL
2 Tbsp	sugar	30 mL
1 tsp	ground nutmeg	5 mL
½ tsp	rum extract	2 mL
½ tsp	vanilla	2 mL
8	ice cubes	8
	Ground nutmeg	

Combine eggs, water, skim milk powder, sugar, 1 tsp (5 mL) nutmeg, rum extract, vanilla and ice cubes in blender container. Cover and blend at high speed until smooth. Pour into cups; sprinkle with nutmeg.

Makes about 3 cups (750 mL).

*Use clean uncracked eggs.

BEVERAGES

Brazilian Breakfast Shake

1 cup	cold milk	250 mL
1	envelope CARNATION Chocolate Instant Breakfast	1
1	small ripe banana, sliced	1
½ tsp	instant coffee granules	2 mL
2	ice cubes	2

Combine milk, instant breakfast, banana, coffee granules and ice cubes in blender container. Cover and blend at high speed until smooth.

Makes about 1¾ cups (425 mL).

O.J. and Cinnamon Smoothie

1 cup	cold milk	250 mL
1	envelope CARNATION Vanilla Instant Breakfast	1
¼ cup	frozen orange juice concentrate	50 mL
	Pinch ground cinnamon	
6	ice cubes	6

Combine milk, instant breakfast, orange juice concentrate, cinnamon and ice cubes in blender container. Cover and blend at high speed until smooth.

Makes about 2½ cups (625 mL).

Peanut Butter 'n' Banana Shake

1 cup	water	250 mL
½ cup	CARNATION Instant Skim Milk Powder	125 mL
¼ cup	peanut butter	50 mL
¼ cup	honey	50 mL
1	medium ripe banana, sliced	1
4	ice cubes	4

Combine water, skim milk powder, peanut butter, honey, banana and ice cubes in blender container. Cover and blend at high speed until smooth.

Makes about 3 cups (750 mL).

Mocha Shake

½ tsp	instant coffee granules	2 mL
¼ cup	hot water	50 mL
2 Tbsp	sugar	30 mL
2 Tbsp	chocolate syrup	30 mL
½ cup	CARNATION Instant Skim Milk Powder	125 mL
6	ice cubes	6

Dissolve coffee in hot water. Combine coffee mixture, sugar, chocolate syrup, skim milk powder and ice cubes in blender container. Cover and blend at high speed until smooth.

Makes about 1¾ cups (425 mL).

Extra Thick Mocha Shake: Add ½ cup (125 mL) vanilla ice cream to Mocha Shake. Blend at high speed 1 min. longer.

Makes about 2 cups (500 mL).

B E V E R A G E S

Carnation
Irish Cream Liqueur

1	can (385 mL) CARNATION 2% Evaporated Milk	1
1 Tbsp	instant coffee granules	15 mL
1 tsp	chocolate syrup	5 mL
2	eggs	2
⅓ cup	sugar	75 mL
½ to ⅔ cup	Irish whiskey	125 to 150 mL

Combine evaporated milk, coffee granules and chocolate syrup in 2-cup (500 mL) glass measure. Microwave, covered, at HIGH (100%) 1½ to 2 min. or until coffee dissolves and mixture is hot. Combine eggs and sugar in 1-quart (1 L) glass measure; beat well. Gradually stir hot liquid into egg mixture. Microwave, covered, at MEDIUM (50%) 2½ to 3 min. or until slightly thickened; stir once while cooking. Blend in whiskey. Cool. Cover and refrigerate.

Makes about 3 cups (750 mL).

B E V E R A G E S

Creamy Swiss Mocha Mix

1 cup	CARNATION Instant Skim Milk Powder	250 mL
⅓ cup	CARNATION Coffee-mate Coffee Whitener	75 mL
¼ cup	instant coffee granules	50 mL
¼ cup	sugar	50 mL
2 Tbsp	unsweetened cocoa powder	30 mL
	Boiling water	

Combine skim milk powder, coffee whitener, coffee granules, sugar and cocoa. For one serving add ¾ cup (175 mL) boiling water to 3 to 4 Tbsp (45 to 60 mL) Creamy Swiss Mocha Mix. For five servings add 4 cups (1 L) boiling water to all the Creamy Swiss Mocha Mix. Creamy Swiss Mocha Mix can be stored in a sealed container and used any time.

Makes 2 cups (500 mL) mix.

Mexican Hot Chocolate

1 cup	CARNATION Instant Skim Milk Powder	250 mL
3 Tbsp	sugar	45 mL
3 Tbsp	unsweetened cocoa powder	45 mL
¼ tsp	ground cinnamon	1 mL
2 cups	water	500 mL
½ tsp	vanilla	2 mL

Combine skim milk powder, sugar, cocoa and cinnamon in small saucepan. Add water. Cook and stir over medium heat until hot and sugar is dissolved. Remove from heat. Stir in vanilla. Beat with wire whisk until frothy.

To Microwave: Combine skim milk powder, sugar, cocoa and cinnamon in 1-quart (1 L) glass measure. Stir in water. Microwave, covered, at HIGH (100%) 1 to 2 min. or until hot. Stir in vanilla. Complete as above.

Makes about 2¼ cups (550 mL).

Savour the flavour...
Beef

"Here are some fast, easy to prepare dishes guaranteed to make the beef lovers at your home smile (they do at mine). These recipes are not only convenient, they're downright delicious."

DINAH CHRISTIE

Dinah Christie is a well-known Canadian entertainer, writer and composer who has appeared in numerous stage and television productions in Canada. Best known for her leading role in "Check it out", Miss Christie is an accomplished comedienne whose infectious laugh and quick wit have been enjoyed by a wide spectrum of Canadian audiences.

Country Oven Stew

1½ lbs	lean stewing beef	750 g
	Flour	
4 Tbsp	vegetable oil, divided	60 mL
1 cup	sliced onion	250 mL
1	can (10 ozs/284 mL) cream of mushroom soup	1
¾ cup	water	175 mL
2 cups	carrot chunks	500 mL
1 cup	*undiluted* CARNATION 2% Evaporated Milk	250 mL
1 cup	frozen cut green beans	250 mL
2 cups	cauliflowerets	500 mL
	Salt and pepper	

Cut meat into bite-size pieces; coat with flour. Brown meat, part at a time in 3 Tbsp (45 mL) hot oil in Dutch oven; set meat aside. Add remaining oil to pan; sauté onion until tender. Return meat to pan. Stir in soup and water. Bake, uncovered, in 350°F (180°C) oven 1 hour. Add carrots. Cover; bake 30 min. longer. Add evaporated milk and beans to stew; top with cauliflowerets. Cover; bake 30 min. longer or until meat and vegetables are cooked. Add salt and pepper to taste.

Makes 5 or 6 servings.

B E E F

Saucy Short Ribs

3 lbs	lean beef short ribs	1.5 kg
	Vegetable oil	
4 cups	diced onions	1000 mL
1	can (10 ozs/284 mL) beef bouillon	1
2½ tsp	seasoned salt	12 mL
1 tsp	Worcestershire sauce	5 mL
¼ tsp	garlic powder	1 mL
¼ tsp	pepper	1 mL
1 cup	*undiluted* CARNATION Evaporated Milk	250 mL
⅓ cup	all purpose flour	75 mL
	Hot cooked noodles	

Trim excess fat from ribs; cut into serving-size pieces. Brown meat, part at a time, in hot oil in large saucepan or Dutch oven; add more oil as needed. Drain excess fat. Add onions, bouillon, salt, Worcestershire sauce, garlic powder and pepper. Bring to boil. Cover and simmer 1½ hours or until meat is tender. Combine evaporated milk and flour until smooth. Stir into meat mixture. Cook and stir over medium heat until mixture comes to a boil and thickens. Serve over hot cooked noodles.

Makes 6 servings.

B E E F

Pot Roast
with Horseradish Sauce

3 lb	pot roast	1.5 kg
	Flour	
2 Tbsp	vegetable oil	30 mL
1	can (10 ozs/284 mL) beef bouillon	1
¼ tsp	dried thyme leaves, crushed	1 mL
1	bay leaf	1
8	small onions, quartered	8
1 cup	*undiluted* CARNATION Evaporated Milk	250 mL
3 Tbsp	flour	45 mL
2 Tbsp	prepared horseradish	30 mL
1 Tbsp	Worcestershire sauce	15 mL
	Salt and pepper	

Coat meat with flour. Brown meat on all sides in hot oil in Dutch oven. Add bouillon, thyme and bay leaf. Bake, covered, in 325°F (160°C) oven 2 hours. Add onions; continue cooking an additional 45 min. or until meat is tender. Remove meat and onions to platter; keep warm. Discard bay leaf. Skim off fat; reserve 2 cups (500 mL) pan liquid. Combine evaporated milk and 3 Tbsp (45 mL) flour until smooth. Add to pan liquid. Cook and stir over medium heat until mixture comes to a boil and thickens. Add horseradish and Worcestershire sauce. Add salt and pepper to taste. Serve sauce with meat and onions.

Makes 6 servings.

B E E F

Burger Pizza

1½ lbs	lean ground beef	750 g
1 cup	fine dry bread crumbs	250 mL
⅔ cup	*undiluted* CARNATION Evaporated Milk	150 mL
1	egg, beaten	1
½ cup	chopped onion	125 mL
1 tsp	salt	5 mL
1	can (7½ ozs/213 mL) pizza sauce	1
2 cups	shredded mozzarella cheese	500 mL
	Pizza toppers: sliced green peppers, mushrooms, olives or chilies	
2 Tbsp	grated Parmesan cheese	30 mL

Combine ground beef, bread crumbs, evaporated milk, egg, onion and salt in large mixing bowl. Mix lightly but thoroughly. Press meat mixture evenly over bottom of 12-inch (30 cm) pizza pan; form a ½-inch (12 mm) rim around edge. Spread pizza sauce over meat. Sprinkle mozzarella cheese and choice of pizza toppers over sauce. Sprinkle with Parmesan cheese. Bake in 350°F (180°C) oven 20 to 25 min. Cut into wedges to serve.

Makes one pizza.

B E E F

Durango Burgers

1 lb	lean ground beef	500 g
½ cup	*undiluted* CARNATION Evaporated Milk	125 mL
1	pkg (35 g) taco seasoning mix	1
4	slices Monterey Jack *or* colby cheese	4
	Shredded lettuce	
	Thinly-sliced tomatoes	
4	hamburger rolls	4
	Taco sauce (optional)	

Combine beef, evaporated milk and taco seasoning; mix lightly but thoroughly. Shape into 4 equal patties; broil or grill 5 inches (12 cm) from source of heat, 4 to 5 min. each side or until cooked as desired. Top with cheese slices; continue cooking until cheese melts. To serve, place lettuce and tomato on bottom half of roll. Top with hamburger patty and top of roll. Serve with taco sauce if desired.

Makes 4 servings.

B E E F

Carnation
Classic Meatloaf

1½ lbs	lean ground beef	750 g
⅔ cup	*undiluted* CARNATION Evaporated Milk	150 mL
½ cup	fine dry bread crumbs	125 mL
½ cup	chopped onion	125 mL
1	egg, beaten	1
1 tsp	garlic salt	5 mL
½ tsp	salt	2 mL

Combine beef, evaporated milk, bread crumbs, onion, egg, garlic salt and salt in large bowl; mix lightly but thoroughly. Place in 8½ x 4½ x 2-inch (1.25 L) loaf pan. Bake in 375°F (190°C) oven 50 to 55 min. Drain. Let stand 10 min. before serving.

To Microwave: Prepare meatloaf as above. Pack into 8½ x 4½ x 2-inch (1.25 L) glass loaf dish. Microwave, covered, at HIGH (100%) 5 min. Drain well. Microwave, covered, at MEDIUM LOW (30%) 35 to 40 min. Let stand, covered, 5 min.; drain.

Makes 6 to 8 servings.

Simply succulent...
Pork

"*Nothing makes me hungrier before dinner than the smell of succulent pork in the oven. If it affects you the same way, look through the next few pages and then get cookin.*"

WHIPPER WATSON

A world-class wrestler, Whipper Watson was twice the World Heavyweight Champion in addition to winning the British Empire title every year from 1943 to 1968. For nearly 40 years, Mr. Watson has associated himself with humanitarian causes such as the fight against MS, and has been accorded both the Order of Canada and the Order of Ontario.

Apple Raisin Pork Chops

8	thin pork chops (about 1½ lbs/750 g)	8
	Flour	
½ tsp	salt	2 mL
2 Tbsp	vegetable oil	30 mL
1 tsp	beef bouillon mix	5 mL
¾ cup	hot water	175 mL
2	large apples, cored, cut in ½-inch (12 mm) wedges	2
½ cup	golden raisins	125 mL
1⅓ cups	*undiluted* CARNATION Evaporated Milk	325 mL
2 Tbsp	flour	30 mL
	Salt and pepper	

Coat pork chops with flour. Sprinkle with ½ tsp (2 mL) salt. Brown chops, part at a time in hot oil in large frypan. Dissolve bouillon mix in hot water; pour over chops. Place apple wedges on chops. Sprinkle raisins over all. Bring to boil. Cover and simmer 25 min. or until chops are tender. Remove chops and apples to heated platter; keep warm. Combine evaporated milk and 2 Tbsp (30 mL) flour until smooth. Stir into drippings in frypan. Cook and stir over medium heat until mixture comes to a boil and thickens. Add salt and pepper to taste. Serve sauce with chops and fruit.

Makes 6 to 8 servings.

Ham 'n' Potato Scallop

6 cups	$^1/_8$-inch (3 mm) thick potato slices	1500 mL
1 cup	thinly-sliced onion	250 mL
2 cups	water	500 mL
1	can (10 ozs/284 mL) cream of mushroom soup	1
1 cup	*undiluted* CARNATION Evaporated Milk	250 mL
1 Tbsp	Dijon mustard	15 mL
1 Tbsp	chopped parsley	15 mL
¼ tsp	pepper	1 mL
2 cups	diced cooked ham	500 mL

Place potatoes, onion and water in large saucepan. Bring to boil. Cover and simmer 5 min. or until barely tender. Drain. Combine soup, evaporated milk, mustard, parsley and pepper. Layer half the potatoes and onions, half the ham and half the soup mixture in greased 2-quart (2 L) shallow baking dish. Repeat layers. Bake in 350°F (180°C) oven 35 to 40 min. or until potatoes are tender and sauce bubbly.

To Microwave: Place potatoes, onion and water in 2½-quart (2.5 L) glass casserole. Microwave, covered, at HIGH (100%) 14 to 15 min. or until potatoes are tender. Drain. Remove half the potato mixture from pan; set aside. Combine soup, evaporated milk, mustard, parsley and pepper. Layer half the ham and half the sauce on potato mixture in casserole. Repeat layering with reserved potato mixture, remaining ham and sauce. Microwave, covered, at MEDIUM HIGH (70%) 10 to 12 min. or until heated through; do not stir.

Makes 6 servings.

P O R K

Pork Tenderloin and Mushrooms Supreme

1 lb	pork tenderloin	500 g
4 Tbsp	butter, divided	60 mL
3 cups	sliced fresh mushrooms	750 mL
½ cup	finely-chopped onion	125 mL
2 Tbsp	flour	30 mL
1 tsp	chicken bouillon mix	5 mL
¼ tsp	dried rosemary leaves, crushed	1 mL
1 cup	*undiluted* CARNATION 2% Evaporated Milk	250 mL
½ cup	water *or* white wine	125 mL
	Salt and pepper	

Cut tenderloin crosswise into ½-inch (12 mm) slices; flatten. Melt 2 Tbsp (30 mL) of the butter in large frypan. Sauté meat, part at a time until browned and cooked through. Remove meat to heated platter; keep warm. Melt remaining 2 Tbsp (30 mL) butter in frypan; sauté mushrooms and onion until tender and any liquid has evaporated. Blend in flour, bouillon mix and rosemary. Gradually stir in evaporated milk and water. Cook and stir over medium heat until mixture comes to a boil and thickens. Add salt and pepper to taste. Pour sauce over meat.

Makes 4 or 5 servings.

P O R K

Yummy
Pork Chop Dinner

6	pork chops (½-inch/12 mm thick)	6
	Salt and pepper	
	Paprika	
2 Tbsp	vegetable oil	30 mL
½ cup	chopped onion	125 mL
¼ cup	chopped green pepper	50 mL
1	can (10 ozs/284 mL) cream of celery soup	1
1 cup	water	250 mL
⅔ cup	*undiluted* CARNATION 2% Evaporated Milk	150 mL
1	can (12 ozs/341 mL) whole kernel corn, drained	1
1 cup	uncooked long grain rice	250 mL
1 tsp	chicken bouillon mix	5 mL
½ tsp	salt	2 mL
¼ tsp	pepper	1 mL

Season pork chops with salt, pepper and paprika. Brown chops, part at a time in hot oil in large frypan. Remove chops. Sauté onion and green pepper until tender. Stir in soup, water, evaporated milk, corn, rice, bouillon mix, ½ tsp (2 mL) salt and ¼ tsp (1 mL) pepper. Pour into 2-quart (2 L) shallow rectangular baking dish. Top with pork chops. Cover and bake in 325°F (160°C) oven 60 min. or until rice is cooked.

Makes 4 to 6 servings.

P O R K

Roasted and Sautéed...

Chicken

"Ask my family what they want for dinner and there's a very good chance the answer will be... CHICKEN!

It seems you can never have too many ways to serve this popular dish. Here are some Peterson favourites that we're sure you will enjoy."

SHELLEY PETERSON

Shelley Peterson is an actress, political wife and mother. She has appeared in over 100 stage productions and most recently co-starred in the CBC production "Not My Department".

Although she leads a hectic life as the wife of David Peterson, premier of Ontario, and the mother of three young children, Mrs. Peterson finds the time to be actively involved with several charitable organizations.

Chicken
Breasts Supreme

1 Tbsp	butter	15 mL
4	boneless skinless chicken breast halves, slightly flattened	4
¼ cup	finely-chopped onion	50 mL
1 tsp	chicken bouillon mix	5 mL
½ tsp	poultry seasoning	2 mL
¼ cup	water	50 mL
¾ cup	*undiluted* CARNATION 2% Evaporated Milk	175 mL
1 Tbsp	flour	15 mL
	Hot cooked noodles	

Melt butter in large frypan. Sauté chicken breasts until golden on both sides; remove from pan. Add onion and sauté until lightly browned. Return chicken to pan. Add bouillon mix and poultry seasoning; pour water over all. Bring to boil. Cover and simmer 10 to 15 min. Remove chicken to heated platter; keep warm. Combine evaporated milk and flour until smooth; stir into pan juices. Cook and stir over medium heat until mixture comes to a boil and thickens. Pour sauce over chicken. Serve with noodles.

Makes 4 servings.

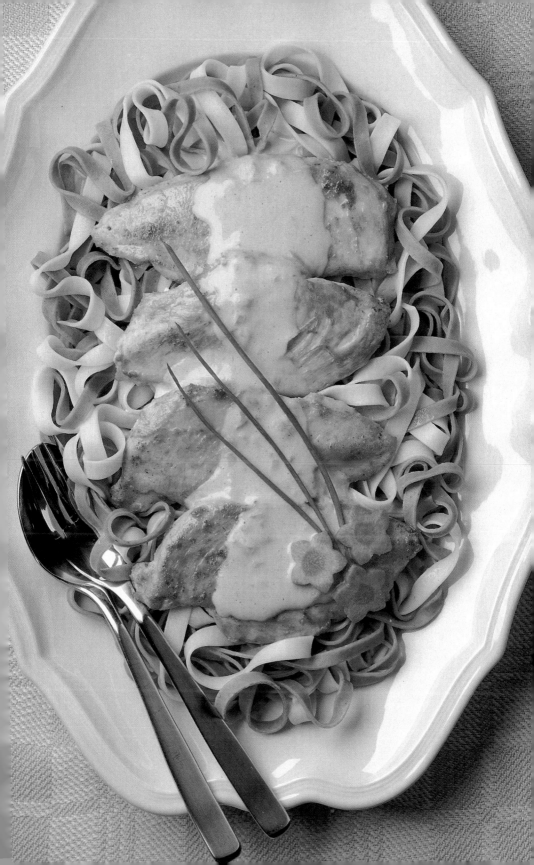

Cornish Game Hens with Toasted Almond Sauce

4	Cornish game hens (1 lb/500 g *each*)	4
½ cup	butter, melted, divided	100 mL
	Salt and pepper	
1	pkg (170 g) long grain and wild rice mix	1
⅔ cup	finely-chopped blanched almonds	150 mL
½ cup	finely-chopped onion	125 mL
2	cloves garlic, crushed, chopped	2
¼ cup	all purpose flour	50 mL
1 Tbsp	chicken bouillon mix	15 mL
1	can (385 mL) CARNATION Evaporated Milk	1
2 cups	water	500 mL
2 Tbsp	chopped parsley	30 mL
	Salt and pepper	

Split game hens in half. Place in roasting pan, breast side up. Brush with ¼ cup (50 mL) of the melted butter. Sprinkle with salt and pepper. Bake in 400°F (200°C) oven 1 hour. Prepare rice mix according to package directions. Sauté almonds in remaining ¼ cup (50 mL) melted butter until golden brown. Add onion and garlic; sauté until tender. Stir in flour and bouillon mix. Gradually stir in evaporated milk and water. Cook and stir over medium heat until mixture comes to a boil and thickens. Stir in parsley. Add salt and pepper to taste. Remove game hens from oven; turn halves over. Fill each cavity with rice. Pour ¼ cup (50 mL) of the sauce over each half. Return to oven; bake 15 min. longer. Keep remaining sauce warm. Serve with game hens.

Makes 8 servings.

Chicken and Carrot Skillet

2 to 3 lbs	chicken pieces	1 to 1.5 kg
	Seasoned salt	
2 Tbsp	vegetable oil	30 mL
1	pkg (35 g) dry onion soup mix	1
2 cups	water	500 mL
4 to 6	peeled carrots	4 to 6
1	can (385 mL) CARNATION Evaporated Milk	1
¼ cup	all purpose flour	50 mL

Sprinkle chicken pieces with seasoned salt. Brown chicken pieces, part at a time in hot oil in large frypan; drain fat. Add soup mix to water; blend well; pour over chicken in pan. Cut carrots in half crosswise. Cut thick end of carrot in half lengthwise; add to frypan. Bring to boil. Cover and simmer 30 to 35 min. or until chicken is tender. Remove chicken and carrots to heated platter; keep warm. Combine evaporated milk and flour until smooth; add to pan. Cook and stir over medium heat until mixture comes to a boil and thickens. Pour gravy over individual servings of chicken and carrots.

Makes 4 servings.

CHICKEN

Piquant
Paprika Chicken

2 Tbsp	butter	30 mL
1 cup	chopped onion	250 mL
1	clove garlic, crushed, chopped	1
2 Tbsp	chicken bouillon mix	30 mL
1 Tbsp	paprika	15 mL
3 lb	chicken, cut up	1.5 kg
1 cup	boiling water	250 mL
⅔ cup	*undiluted* CARNATION Evaporated Milk	150 mL
3 Tbsp	flour	45 mL
¾ cup	yogurt *or* sour cream	175 mL
	Salt and pepper	

Melt butter in Dutch oven. Sauté onion and garlic until tender. Blend in bouillon mix and paprika. Add chicken pieces. Pour water over all. Bring to boil. Cover and simmer 25 min. or until chicken is tender. Remove chicken pieces to heated platter; keep warm. Combine evaporated milk and flour until smooth; add to pan. Cook and stir over medium heat until mixture comes to a boil and thickens. Gradually stir in yogurt. Add salt and pepper to taste. Spoon some of the sauce over chicken and pass remainder as gravy.

Makes 4 or 5 servings.

Family Chicken Stew

4 lbs	chicken pieces	2 kg
2 cups	water	500 mL
1 Tbsp	chicken bouillon mix	15 mL
1 tsp	salt	5 mL
1 tsp	poultry seasoning	5 mL
2 cups	thinly-sliced carrots	500 mL
2 cups	peeled diced potatoes	500 mL
1 cup	sliced celery	250 mL
5	small onions, quartered	5
1	can (385 mL) CARNATION 2% Evaporated Milk	1
½ cup	all purpose flour	125 mL
1½ cups	frozen peas	375 mL
	Salt and pepper	

Combine chicken pieces, water, bouillon mix, 1 tsp (5 mL) salt and poultry seasoning in large saucepan. Bring to boil. Cover and simmer 45 min. to 1 hour or until chicken is tender. Remove chicken. Add carrots, potatoes, celery and onion to pan. Cover and simmer 20 min. or until vegetables are just tender. Remove skin and bones from chicken; cut chicken into bite-size pieces. Combine evaporated milk and flour until smooth; add to pan. Add peas. Cook and stir over medium heat until mixture comes to a boil and thickens. Add salt and pepper to taste. Return cut-up chicken to pan. Reheat to serving temperature if necessary.

Makes 6 to 8 servings.

Chicken Fricassee

1	chicken (3½ to 4 lbs/1.75 to 2 kg), cut up	1
½ cup	chopped onion	125 mL
1⅓ cups	water	325 mL
2 tsp	chicken bouillon mix	10 mL
¼ tsp	dried rosemary leaves, crushed	1 mL
¼ tsp	dried marjoram leaves, crushed	1 mL
2	whole cloves	2
1	can (385 mL) CARNATION Evaporated Milk	1
¼ cup	all purpose flour	50 mL
2 tsp	lemon juice	10 mL
	Salt and pepper	
	6-serving recipe CARNATION Instant Mashed Potatoes	

Place chicken pieces in large saucepan. Add onion, water, bouillon mix, rosemary, marjoram and cloves. Bring to boil. Cover and simmer 45 min. or until chicken is tender. Remove chicken pieces to heated platter; keep warm. Discard cloves. Combine evaporated milk and flour until smooth; stir into pan juices. Cook and stir over medium heat until mixture comes to a boil and thickens. Add lemon juice. Add salt and pepper to taste. Pour sauce over chicken; keep warm. Prepare mashed potatoes according to package directions. Serve with chicken and sauce.

To Microwave: Arrange chicken pieces with meaty portions toward outside of 3-quart (3 L) shallow glass casserole. Add onion, water, bouillon mix, rosemary, marjoram and cloves. Microwave, covered, at HIGH (100%) 24 to 26 min. or until chicken is tender; turn pieces over once while cooking. Remove chicken; keep warm. Discard cloves. Combine evaporated milk and flour until smooth; stir into pan juices. Microwave, uncovered, at HIGH (100%) 4 to 5 min. or until sauce boils and thickens; stir 4 times while cooking. Add lemon juice. Add salt and pepper to taste. Complete as above.

Makes 5 or 6 servings.

Tender and tasty...
Fish

"Anyone born in Charlottetown, P.E.I. knows how to enjoy the great taste of fish. I'm no exception! When you think about the many different types of fresh fish Canadians are able to choose from and the unique ways to prepare and serve fish, how can anyone resist? I fished around for a few of my best picks. Here they are."

JOE GHIZ

Premier Ghiz has enjoyed a career as a senior partner in a Charlottetown law firm, during which he served as president of the Prince Edward Island Branch of the Canadian Bar Association.

Active in the community, Mr. Ghiz has lectured at the University of Prince Edward Island and is a founding member of the Montague Boys and Girls Club.

He became leader of the provincial Liberal Party in 1981 and became provincial premier in 1986.

Parmesan Baked Sole

2 lbs	sole fillets (thawed if frozen)	1 kg
½ tsp	salt	2 mL
3 Tbsp	lemon juice *or* white wine	45 mL
2 Tbsp	finely-chopped green onions	30 mL
3 Tbsp	butter	45 mL
3 Tbsp	flour	45 mL
1 tsp	chicken bouillon mix	5 mL
1 cup	*undiluted* CARNATION 2% Evaporated Milk	250 mL
½ cup	water	125 mL
¼ cup	grated Parmesan cheese	50 mL
	Salt and pepper	
1 cup	small cooked shrimp (optional)	250 mL
	Hot cooked rice	

Roll up fillets and secure with toothpicks. Place in single layer in 1½-quart (1.5 L) shallow glass baking dish. Sprinkle with ½ tsp (2 mL) salt, lemon juice and onions. Cover; bake in 400°F (200°C) oven 20 min. or until fish flakes easily with fork. Drain fish reserving ½ cup (125 mL) of pan liquid. Melt butter in saucepan. Blend in flour and bouillon mix. Gradually stir in evaporated milk, water and reserved pan liquid. Cook and stir over medium heat until mixture comes to a boil and thickens. Stir in cheese. Add salt and pepper to taste. Add shrimp if desired. Pour sauce over fish. Bake an additional 10 to 15 min. Serve with rice.

Makes 6 servings.

F I S H

Quick Fish Bake with Hot Tartar Sauce

1	pkg (454 g) frozen fish fillets*	1
	Butter	
	Lemon juice	
2 Tbsp	butter	30 mL
2 Tbsp	finely-chopped onion	30 mL
2 Tbsp	flour	30 mL
1 cup	*undiluted* CARNATION 2% Evaporated Milk	250 mL
½ cup	water	125 mL
¼ cup	mayonnaise *or* salad dressing	50 mL
3 Tbsp	sweet pickle relish	45 mL
1 Tbsp	lemon juice	15 mL
	Few drops hot pepper sauce	
	Salt and pepper	
	Hot cooked rice	

With a serrated knife cut block of frozen fish crosswise into 4 equal pieces. Place in greased 1½-quart (1.5 L) shallow glass baking dish. Dot with butter; sprinkle with lemon juice. Bake in 450°F (230°C) oven 20 to 25 min. or until fish flakes easily with fork. Meanwhile melt 2 Tbsp (30 mL) butter in small saucepan. Sauté onion until tender. Blend in flour. Gradually stir in evaporated milk and water. Cook and stir over medium heat until mixture comes to a boil and thickens. Stir in mayonnaise, relish, 1 Tbsp (15 mL) lemon juice and hot pepper sauce. Add salt and pepper to taste. Reheat to serving temperature. Drain fish; place on bed of rice. Pour sauce over all.

Makes 4 servings.

*Do not use individually frozen fillets.

F I S H

Haddock Florentine

4 Tbsp	butter, divided	60 mL
1	medium onion, thinly sliced	1
2	pkgs (300 g *each*) frozen chopped spinach, thawed, squeezed dry	2
1	can (10 ozs/284 mL) sliced mushrooms, drained	1
1	pkg (454 g) frozen haddock fillets, thawed	1
½ tsp	salt	2 mL
¼ tsp	dried thyme leaves, crushed	1 mL
⅔ cup	*undiluted* CARNATION Evaporated Milk	150 mL
2 Tbsp	flour	30 mL
	Salt and pepper	

Melt 2 Tbsp (30 mL) of the butter in medium frypan. Sauté onion until tender. Add spinach and mushrooms to pan. Place fish fillets on top of spinach; dot with remaining 2 Tbsp (30 mL) butter. Sprinkle with ½ tsp (2 mL) salt and thyme. Cover and cook over low heat until fish flakes easily with fork, about 15 min. Remove fish to heated platter; keep warm. Combine evaporated milk and flour until smooth; stir into spinach. Cook and stir over medium heat until mixture comes to a boil and thickens. Add salt and pepper to taste. Spoon spinach mixture onto serving plate; top with fish fillets.

To Microwave: Combine 2 Tbsp (30 mL) of the butter and onion in 2-quart (2 L) shallow glass baking dish. Microwave, uncovered, at HIGH (100%) 3 to 4 min. or until onion is tender; stir twice while cooking. Add mushrooms and spinach. Place fish fillets on top of spinach mixture; dot with remaining 2 Tbsp (30 mL) butter. Sprinkle with ½ tsp (2 mL) salt and thyme. Microwave, covered, at HIGH (100%) 6 to 7 min. or until fish flakes easily with fork. Remove fish to heated platter; keep warm. Combine evaporated milk and flour until smooth; stir into spinach. Microwave, uncovered, at HIGH (100%) 2 to 3 min. or until mixture boils and thickens; stir once while cooking. Add salt and pepper to taste. Complete as above.

Makes 4 servings.

F I S H

Cheddar Cod Bake

2 Tbsp	butter	30 mL
2 Tbsp	flour	30 mL
¾ tsp	dry mustard	3 mL
⅔ cup	*undiluted* CARNATION Evaporated Milk	150 mL
⅓ cup	water	75 mL
1½ cups	shredded Cheddar cheese	375 mL
	Salt and pepper	
1	pkg (454 g) frozen cod fillets, thawed	1
2 Tbsp	chopped parsley	30 mL

Melt butter in saucepan. Blend in flour and dry mustard. Gradually stir in evaporated milk and water. Cook and stir over medium heat until mixture comes to a boil and thickens. Add cheese; stir until melted. Add salt and pepper to taste. Spread half the sauce in 1½-quart (1.5 L) shallow glass baking dish. Cut cod into serving-size pieces. Arrange on top of sauce. Spread remaining sauce over fish; sprinkle with parsley. Bake in 400°F (200°C) oven 20 to 25 min. or until fish flakes easily with fork. To serve, remove fish; stir sauce; pour over fish.

To Microwave: Place butter in 1-quart (1 L) glass measure. Microwave, uncovered, at HIGH (100%) 45 sec. Blend in flour and mustard. Gradually stir in evaporated milk and water. Microwave, uncovered, at HIGH (100%) 3 to 4 min. or until sauce boils and thickens; stir 3 times while cooking. Add cheese; stir until melted. Add salt and pepper to taste. Arrange sauce and fish as above. Microwave, covered, at MEDIUM HIGH (70%) 4 to 5 min. or until fish flakes easily with fork. Complete as above.

Makes 4 servings.

F I S H

Creamy, Fresh and Wholesome…

Eggs & Cheese

"I enjoy foods that are fresh and natural, prepared carefully and served with simplicity. The following pages feature a few such dishes. They're really quite easy to prepare, yet they look exquisite and taste even better."

GORDON PINSENT

Gordon Pinsent is an acclaimed actor, writer and director. With credits such as director of "John and the Missus," star of "The Rowdy Man," writer and star of "A Gift to Last" and star of "Quentin Durgens," he is the highly deserving winner of two Genies and two Nellies.

Easy
Cheese Souffle

2 Tbsp	butter	30 mL
2 Tbsp	flour	30 mL
¼ tsp	pepper	1 mL
	Pinch dry mustard	
	Pinch cayenne	
¾ cup	*undiluted* CARNATION Evaporated Milk	175 mL
2 cups	shredded 'old' Cheddar cheese	500 mL
4	eggs, (at room temperature), separated	4
¼ tsp	cream of tartar	1 mL

Melt butter in medium saucepan. Blend in flour, pepper, dry mustard and cayenne. Gradually stir in evaporated milk. Cook and stir over medium heat until mixture comes to a boil and thickens. Add cheese; stir until melted. Beat egg yolks slightly; stir into cheese mixture. Beat egg whites with cream of tartar in large mixer bowl until stiff but not dry. Gently fold beaten egg whites into cheese mixture. Spoon into 2-quart (2 L) soufflé dish. For a "top hat," trace a circle through mixture with a spoon 1-inch (2.5 cm) from edge. Bake in 350°F (180°C) oven 35 to 40 min. Serve immediately.

Makes 4 servings.

Eggs
Florentine

4	slices chopped bacon	4
¼ cup	finely-chopped onion	50 mL
2 Tbsp	flour	30 mL
¾ cup	*undiluted* CARNATION 2% Evaporated Milk	175 mL
¼ cup	water	50 mL
¼ cup	grated Parmesan cheese	50 mL
1	pkg (300 g) frozen chopped spinach, thawed, squeezed dry	1
	Salt and pepper	
4	eggs	4
¼ cup	shredded Swiss cheese	50 mL

Cook bacon in medium saucepan until crisp. Drain well, reserving drippings; set bacon aside. Sauté onion in bacon drippings until tender. Blend in flour. Gradually stir in evaporated milk and water. Cook and stir over medium heat until mixture comes to a boil and thickens. Stir in Parmesan cheese and spinach. Add salt and pepper to taste. Divide spinach mixture among four 10-oz (300 mL) custard cups. Make a depression in the centre of each. Break an egg into each depression. Sprinkle equal amounts of Swiss cheese then reserved bacon on top of each egg. Bake in 325°F (160°C) oven about 15 min. or until eggs are cooked as desired. Serve immediately.

Makes 4 servings.

EGGS AND CHEESE

Prepare Ahead Brunch Eggs

5 Tbsp	butter, divided	75 mL
3 Tbsp	flour	45 mL
1	can (385 mL) CARNATION 2% Evaporated Milk	1
⅓ cup	water	75 mL
1½ cups	shredded 'old' Cheddar cheese	375 mL
	Salt and pepper	
1 cup	sliced fresh mushrooms	250 mL
¼ cup	finely-chopped onion	50 mL
12	eggs, beaten	12
1 cup	fresh bread crumbs	250 mL

Melt 2 Tbsp (30 mL) of the butter in saucepan. Blend in flour. Gradually stir in evaporated milk and water. Cook and stir over medium heat until mixture comes to a boil and thickens. Remove from heat. Add cheese and stir until melted. Add salt and pepper to taste. Cover and set aside. Melt 2 more Tbsp (30 mL) of the butter in large frypan. Sauté mushrooms and onion until tender and any liquid has evaporated. Add eggs and continue cooking and stirring until mixture is just set. Stir cheese sauce into eggs. Pour into 1½-quart (1.5 L) shallow rectangular baking dish. Melt remaining 1 Tbsp (15 mL) butter. Toss with bread crumbs. Sprinkle over egg and sauce mixture. Cover and refrigerate overnight. Bake, uncovered, in 350°F (180°C) oven 20 to 25 min. or until heated through.

Makes 6 to 8 servings.

Carnation
Classic Quiche

8	slices crisp crumbled bacon	8
1	(9-inch/23 cm) unbaked pastry shell	1
2 cups	shredded Swiss cheese	500 mL
4	eggs, beaten	4
1	can (385 mL) CARNATION Evaporated Milk	1
2 Tbsp	minced onion	30 mL
1 tsp	Worcestershire sauce	5 mL
½ tsp	salt	2 mL
1 Tbsp	grated Parmesan cheese	15 mL

Sprinkle bacon over bottom of unbaked pastry shell. Cover with Swiss cheese. Combine eggs, evaporated milk, onion, Worcestershire sauce and salt; mix well. Pour into pastry shell. Sprinkle with Parmesan cheese. Bake in 375°F (190°C) oven 30 to 35 min. or until knife inserted near centre comes out clean. Let stand 5 min. before serving.

Makes one quiche.

E G G S   A N D   C H E E S E

Pizza Oven Omelet

1 Tbsp	butter	15 mL
1 cup	sliced fresh mushrooms	250 mL
2 Tbsp	finely-diced green pepper	30 mL
6	eggs	6
1 cup	*undiluted* CARNATION Evaporated Milk	250 mL
½ tsp	seasoned salt	2 mL
4 ozs	mozzarella cheese, thinly sliced	125 g
1	can (7½ ozs/213 mL) pizza sauce	1

Melt butter in small frypan. Sauté mushrooms and green pepper until tender and any liquid has evaporated. Combine eggs, evaporated milk and salt in bowl; beat until well combined; stir in mushroom mixture. Pour into buttered 9-inch (23 cm) pie plate. Bake in 350°F (180°C) oven 20 to 25 min. Top with cheese slices. Bake 5 min. longer or until cheese is melted. Heat pizza sauce. Spoon sauce over servings of omelet.

To Microwave: Place butter, mushrooms and green pepper in 9-inch (23 cm) glass pie plate. Microwave, uncovered, at HIGH (100%) 4 min. or until vegetables are tender; stir twice while cooking. Combine eggs, evaporated milk and salt in bowl; beat well. Stir into vegetables. Microwave, covered, at MEDIUM HIGH (70%) 4½ to 5 min. or until partially set. Lift cooked eggs to allow uncooked centre to flow to outside edge. Microwave, uncovered, at MEDIUM HIGH (70%) 2 to 3 min. or until almost set. Top with cheese. Cover and let stand 1 to 2 min. or until cheese melts. Place pizza sauce in small glass bowl. Microwave, covered, at HIGH (100%) 1½ min. or until hot; stir once while heating. Complete as above.

Makes 4 or 5 servings.

EGGS AND CHEESE

Pinwheel Cheese Pie

5	eggs, beaten	5
1½ cups	shredded Cheddar cheese	375 mL
⅔ cup	*undiluted* CARNATION 2% Evaporated Milk	150 mL
⅓ cup	water	75 mL
1 Tbsp	finely-chopped green onion	15 mL
8	slices day-old bread	8
	Butter, softened	
6	slices crisp crumbled bacon	6

Combine eggs, cheese, evaporated milk, water and green onion. Pour into buttered 9-inch (23 cm) pie plate. Trim crusts from bread; lightly butter bread. Cut each slice of bread in half diagonally. Place bread triangles in egg mixture overlapping, as in a pinwheel. Sprinkle bacon over bread. Bake in 350°F (180°C) oven 40 to 45 min. or until knife inserted near centre comes out clean.

Makes one pie.

Add a little something special…

Vegetables & Side Dishes

"Most good cooks will admit that the main dish may first attract the diner's attention but, it's the subtle touches surrounding the main dish that result in the most pleasurable dining experience. Here are but a few side and vegetable dishes that can add a crowning touch to your next culinary outing."

CHANTAL DEVINE

Chantal Devine is an accomplished school teacher. Mother of five, she is the wife of D. Grant Devine, the present premier of Saskatchewan. Mrs. Devine's involvement in several community organizations reflects both her public role as wife of the premier and her personal areas of interest and concern. She serves as a provincial ambassador for the Multiple Sclerosis Society.

Carnation Classic Cheese Sauce for Vegetables

2 Tbsp	butter	30 mL
2 Tbsp	chopped green onions	30 mL
1 Tbsp	flour	15 mL
	Few grains cayenne	
¾ cup	*undiluted* CARNATION Evaporated Milk	175 mL
¼ cup	water	50 mL
1 cup	shredded 'old' Cheddar cheese	250 mL
	Salt and pepper	
	Assorted hot cooked vegetables	
	(green beans, broccoli, cauliflower, etc.)	

Melt butter in medium saucepan. Sauté onions until tender. Blend in flour and cayenne. Gradually stir in evaporated milk and water. Cook and stir over medium heat until mixture comes to a boil and thickens. Add cheese; stir until melted. Add salt and pepper to taste. Serve sauce over hot cooked vegetables.

To Microwave: Combine butter and onions in 1-quart (1 L) glass measure. Microwave, uncovered, at HIGH (100%) 1 to 1½ min. or until onions are tender; stir once while cooking. Blend in flour and cayenne. Gradually stir in evaporated milk and water. Microwave, uncovered, at HIGH (100%) 3 to 4 min. or until sauce boils and thickens; stir three times while cooking. Add cheese; stir until melted. Add salt and pepper to taste. Complete as above.

Makes about 1⅓ cups (325 mL) sauce.

Spinach Rice au Gratin

2 Tbsp	butter	30 mL
½ cup	chopped onion	125 mL
1	clove garlic, crushed, chopped	1
1 Tbsp	flour	15 mL
½ tsp	chicken bouillon mix	2 mL
1 cup	*undiluted* CARNATION 2% Evaporated Milk	250 mL
⅓ cup	water	75 mL
1 cup	shredded Cheddar cheese	250 mL
1	pkg (300 g) frozen chopped spinach, thawed, squeezed dry	1
1½ cups	cooked rice	375 mL
	Salt and pepper	
	Buttered Bread Crumbs	

Melt butter in medium saucepan. Sauté onion and garlic until tender. Blend in flour and bouillon mix. Gradually stir in evaporated milk and water. Cook and stir over medium heat until mixture comes to a boil and thickens. Remove from heat. Add cheese; stir until melted. Stir in spinach and rice. Add salt and pepper to taste. Spoon into 1-quart (1 L) casserole. Top with Buttered Bread Crumbs. Bake in 375°F (190°C) oven 20 to 25 min.

Buttered Bread Crumbs: Toss ½ cup (125 mL) fresh bread crumbs with 1 Tbsp (15 mL) melted butter.

To Microwave: Combine butter, onion and garlic in 1-quart (1 L) glass measure. Microwave, uncovered, at HIGH (100%) 4 to 4½ min. or until onion is tender; stir twice while cooking. Blend in flour and bouillon mix. Gradually stir in evaporated milk and water. Microwave, uncovered, at HIGH (100%) 4 to 5 min. or until sauce boils and thickens; stir 3 times while cooking. Add cheese; stir until melted. Stir in spinach and rice. Add salt and pepper to taste. Omit Buttered Bread Crumbs. Microwave, covered, at HIGH (100%) 2 min. or until heated through; stir once while cooking.

Makes 5 or 6 servings.

VEGETABLES AND SIDE DISHES

Three Bean Chili Bake

3	slices bacon, halved	3
1½ cups	coarsely-chopped onions	375 mL
1 Tbsp	flour	15 mL
⅓ cup	bottled chili sauce	75 mL
3 Tbsp	molasses	45 mL
1 Tbsp	prepared mustard	15 mL
⅔ cup	*undiluted* CARNATION 2% Evaporated Milk	150 mL
1	can (14 ozs/398 mL) cut waxed beans, drained	1
1	can (14 ozs/398 mL) kidney beans, rinsed, drained	1
1	can (14 ozs/398 mL)cut green beans, drained	1
	Salt and pepper	

Cook bacon in large frypan until crisp. Drain reserving 2 Tbsp (30 mL) drippings. Set bacon aside. Sauté onion in reserved drippings. Blend in flour, chili sauce, molasses and mustard. Gradually stir in evaporated milk. Add waxed, kidney and green beans. Spoon into 1½-quart (1.5 L) shallow rectangular baking dish. Bake in 350°F (180°C) oven 25 min. or until hot. Add salt and pepper to taste. Arrange bacon pieces on top. Bake 5 min. longer.

To Microwave: Place bacon in 1½-quart (1.5 L) shallow rectangular glass baking dish. Microwave, loosely covered, at HIGH (100%) 4 to 5 min. or until bacon is crisp; turn once while cooking. Set bacon aside; reserve 2 Tbsp (30 mL) drippings. Add onions to reserved drippings. Microwave, uncovered, at HIGH (100%) 4 to 5 min. or until onions are tender; stir twice while cooking. Blend in flour, chili sauce, molasses and mustard. Gradually stir in evaporated milk. Add waxed, kidney and green beans. Microwave, covered, at HIGH (100%) 4 min. or until heated through; stir twice while cooking. Add salt and pepper to taste. Arrange bacon slices on top. Microwave, uncovered, at HIGH (100%) 1 min.

Makes 6 to 8 servings.

Carrots 'n' Green Beans in Creamy Bacon Sauce

3	slices bacon, diced	3
½ cup	chopped onion	125 mL
½ cup	sliced celery	125 mL
2 cups	carrot sticks	500 mL
2 cups	cut fresh green beans	500 mL
1 tsp	chicken bouillon mix	5 mL
½ cup	water	125 mL
⅔ cup	*undiluted* CARNATION 2% Evaporated Milk	150 mL
1 Tbsp	flour	15 mL

Cook bacon in large frypan until almost crisp. Add onion and celery to bacon; cook until tender. Add carrots, beans and bouillon mix to pan. Pour water over all. Bring to boil. Cover and simmer 10 min. or until vegetables are crisp-tender. Combine evaporated milk and flour until smooth. Stir into vegetable mixture. Cook and stir over medium heat until mixture comes to a boil and thickens.

To Microwave: Place bacon in 3-quart (3 L) shallow glass baking dish. Microwave, loosely covered, at HIGH (100%) 4 min. or until almost crisp. Add onion and celery. Microwave, covered, at HIGH (100%) 3 min. or until vegetables are tender; stir once while cooking. Add carrots, beans and bouillon mix. Pour water over all. Microwave, covered, at HIGH (100%) 13 min. or until vegetables are crisp-tender; stir three times while cooking. Combine evaporated milk and flour until smooth. Stir into vegetable mixture. Microwave, uncovered, at HIGH (100%) 2 min. or until sauce boils and thickens; stir once while cooking.

Makes about 4 cups (1 L).

Enjoy the aroma of home...
Baking

"My mother always told me that I should finish everything on my plate. Actually, cleaning my plate was the fastest way to get to mom's baking. As far as I'm concerned, it's the best part of any meal."

HARVEY KIRCK

Harvey Kirck is a well-known Canadian broadcaster who spent more than two decades co-anchoring the CTV National News. Mr. Kirck's direct and frank coverage of the news has earned him a special place in the minds and hearts of millions of Canadian TV viewers.

Cheddar Nugget Bread

6 tsp	sugar, divided	30 mL
½ cup	lukewarm water	125 mL
1	envelope dry granular yeast	1
1 cup	*undiluted* CARNATION 2% Evaporated Milk	250 mL
2 Tbsp	butter, melted	30 mL
1½ tsp	salt	7 mL
3½ to 4 cups	all purpose flour	750 to 1000 mL
1½ cups	shredded 'old' Cheddar cheese	375 mL

Dissolve 2 tsp (10 mL) of the sugar in lukewarm water in large bowl. Stir in yeast; let stand 10 min.; stir well. Add evaporated milk, butter, remaining 4 tsp (20 mL) sugar and salt. Stir in about 3 cups (750 mL) flour to make stiff dough. Turn out onto floured board. Knead until elastic, working in additional flour, about 8 min. Place in buttered bowl turning dough to butter top. Cover; let rise in warm place until double in bulk, about 1 hour. Punch dough down. Turn out on lightly floured board. Roll out to 14 x 12-inch (35 x 30 cm) rectangle. Sprinkle cheese over surface of dough. Roll up jelly roll-style starting at long end; cut roll into 1-inch (2.5 cm) sections. Cut each section into quarters. Divide the pieces of dough evenly between two foil-lined 8½ x 4½ x 2½-inch (1.25 L) loaf pans. (Do not let cut surfaces of dough touch sides or bottoms of pans.) Cover; let rise in warm place until double in bulk, about 1 hour. Bake in 375°F (190°C) oven 25 to 30 min. or until done. Remove from pans at once; cool on wire racks.

Makes 2 loaves.

BAKING

Peanut Butter Crunchies

½ cup	butter, softened	125 mL
½ cup	smooth peanut butter	125 mL
¾ cup	packed brown sugar	175 mL
1	egg	1
1 tsp	vanilla	5 mL
1 cup	quick cooking rolled oats	250 mL
¾ cup	whole wheat flour	175 mL
½ cup	CARNATION Instant Skim Milk Powder	125 mL
½ tsp	salt	2 mL
¼ tsp	baking powder	1 mL
¼ tsp	baking soda	1 mL
1 cup	finely-chopped peanuts	250 mL

Cream butter, peanut butter, sugar, egg and vanilla in large mixer bowl until light and fluffy. Combine oats, flour, skim milk powder, salt, baking powder and baking soda. Stir into creamed mixture. Add peanuts. Drop by small spoonfuls onto lightly greased cookie sheets. Flatten each cookie with the bottom of a glass dipped in sugar. Bake in 375°F (190°C) oven 8 to 9 min.

Makes 4 dozen.

Apple Spice Muffins

3 cups	all purpose flour	750 mL
1⅓ cups	CARNATION Instant Skim Milk Powder	325 mL
⅔ cup	sugar	150 mL
4 tsp	baking powder	20 mL
1 tsp	ground cinnamon	5 mL
1 tsp	salt	5 mL
2	eggs	2
1 cup	apple juice	250 mL
½ cup	butter, melted	125 mL
2 cups	finely-chopped pared apple	500 mL
	Sugar	
	Cinnamon Apple Butter	

Stir together flour, skim milk powder, sugar, baking powder, cinnamon and salt in large bowl. Beat eggs and apple juice in medium bowl; blend in butter and apple. Add to dry ingredients all at once; stir just until moistened. Divide batter among 12 large greased muffin cups (muffin cups will be full). Sprinkle muffins with sugar. Bake in 375°F (190°C) oven 25 to 30 min. Serve warm with Cinnamon Apple Butter.

Makes 12 large muffins.

Cinnamon Apple Butter: Cream ½ cup (125 mL) softened butter. Beat in ⅓ cup (75 mL) apple jelly and ¼ tsp (1 mL) ground cinnamon.

Makes about 1 cup (250 mL).

BAKING

Banana Split Cookies

1 cup	butter, softened	250 mL
1 cup	sugar	250 mL
2	eggs	2
1 cup	mashed ripe bananas	250 mL
½ cup	*undiluted* CARNATION Evaporated Milk	125 mL
1 Tbsp	vinegar	15 mL
1 tsp	vanilla	5 mL
2⅔ cups	all purpose flour	650 mL
1½ tsp	baking soda	7 mL
½ tsp	salt	2 mL
1 cup	chopped nuts	250 mL
	Butterscotch Frosting	
	Maraschino cherry halves	

Beat together butter, sugar, eggs, bananas, evaporated milk, vinegar
and vanilla in large mixer bowl until smoothly combined. Stir
together flour, baking soda and salt in medium bowl. Add dry
ingredients to banana mixture all at once; stir just until moistened.
Stir in nuts. Drop dough by rounded spoonfuls, 2 inches (5 cm)
apart on lightly greased cookie sheets. Bake in 375°F (190°C) oven
15 to 18 min. Cool on wire racks. Frost with Butterscotch Frosting.
Top with maraschino cherry halves.

Butterscotch Frosting: Melt 6 Tbsp (90 mL) butter in small saucepan.
Add ¾ cup (175 mL) packed brown sugar. Boil 1 min.; stir constantly.
Remove from heat; cool slightly. Stir in 3 Tbsp (45 mL) *undiluted*
CARNATION Evaporated Milk. Beat in ½ cup (125 mL) sifted icing
sugar until smooth. Spoon over cookies.

Makes about 3½ dozen.

B A K I N G

Pumpkin Spice Cake

¾ cup	butter, softened	175 mL
1½ cups	sugar	375 mL
3	eggs	3
1½ cups	canned pumpkin	375 mL
1½ tsp	vanilla	7 mL
3 cups	all purpose flour	750 mL
3½ tsp	baking powder	17 mL
1 tsp	baking soda	5 mL
¾ tsp	salt	4 mL
1½ tsp	ground cinnamon	7 mL
¾ tsp	ground nutmeg	4 mL
¼ tsp	ground cloves	1 mL
¼ tsp	ground ginger	1 mL
¾ cup	*undiluted* CARNATION Evaporated Milk	175 mL
	Icing sugar	

Cream butter and sugar until light in large mixer bowl. Add eggs, one at a time, beating well after each addition. Blend in pumpkin and vanilla. Stir together flour, baking powder, baking soda, salt and spices. Add dry ingredients to creamed mixture alternately with evaporated milk, combining lightly after each addition. Turn batter into greased 12-cup (3 L) Bundt pan or 10-inch (25 cm) tube pan. Bake in 350°F (180°C) oven 55 to 60 min. Cool in pan 10 min.; remove from pan. Cool completely. Dust with icing sugar.

Makes one ring cake.

BAKING

Cherry Streusel Coffeecake

2¼ cups	all purpose flour	550 mL
¾ cup	sugar	175 mL
¾ cup	butter	175 mL
½ tsp	baking powder	2 mL
½ tsp	baking soda	2 mL
¾ cup	*undiluted* CARNATION Evaporated Milk	175 mL
1 Tbsp	lemon juice	15 mL
1	egg	1
1	can (19 ozs/540 mL) cherry pie filling	1

Stir together flour and sugar in large bowl. Cut in butter with pastry blender until mixture resembles coarse crumbs; set aside ½ cup (125 mL) of mixture. To remainder add baking powder and baking soda. Combine evaporated milk and lemon juice. Add egg; beat well. Add evaporated milk mixture to dry ingredients all at once; stir just until moistened. Spread two-thirds of batter over bottom and part way up side of greased 9-inch (23 cm) springform pan. Spread cherry pie filling over top; spoon remaining batter in small mounds over pie filling; sprinkle with reserved crumb mixture. Bake in 350°F (180°C) oven 45 to 50 min. Serve warm.

Makes 1 cake.

Blueberry Cobbler

½ cup	sugar	125 mL
1 Tbsp	corn starch	15 mL
4 cups	fresh blueberries*	1000 mL
1 tsp	lemon juice	5 mL
1½ cups	all purpose flour	375 mL
½ cup	CARNATION Instant Skim Milk Powder	125 mL
3 Tbsp	sugar	45 mL
2½ tsp	baking powder	7 mL
½ tsp	salt	2 mL
⅓ cup	butter	75 mL
¾ cup	water	175 mL
	Custard Sauce	

Combine ½ cup (125 mL) sugar, corn starch, blueberries and lemon juice in saucepan. Cook and stir over medium heat until mixture comes to a boil and thickens. Cover. Stir together flour, skim milk powder, 3 Tbsp (45 mL) sugar, baking powder and salt. Cut in butter with pastry blender until mixture resembles coarse crumbs. Add water; stir just until blended. Reheat fruit mixture to boiling; pour into 2-quart (2 L) shallow rectangular baking dish. Drop spoonfuls of batter over fruit mixture. Bake in 400°F (200°C) oven 25 to 30 min. or until done. Serve warm with Custard Sauce.

Makes 6 servings.

Custard Sauce: Combine ¼ cup (50 mL) CARNATION Instant Skim Milk Powder, 2 Tbsp (30 mL) sugar and 4 tsp (20 mL) corn starch in medium saucepan. Stir in 1 cup (250 mL) water. Cook and stir over medium heat until mixture comes to a boil and thickens. Reduce heat; cook 1 min. longer. Remove from heat; beat small amount of hot mixture into 1 beaten egg yolk. Stir egg mixture back into saucepan. Cook and stir until sauce thickens. Remove from heat. Stir in 2 Tbsp (30 mL) butter and 1 tsp (5 mL) vanilla. Cover surface with plastic warp. Serve warm or cool.

Makes about 1¼ cups (300 mL).

*Or use 2 pkgs (300 g *each*) frozen blueberries.

BAKING

Chocolate Caramel Brownies

1	pkg (520 g) chocolate cake mix	1
½ cup	butter	125 mL
1 cup	finely-chopped nuts	250 mL
½ cup	*undiluted* CARNATION Evaporated Milk	125 mL
35	individually wrapped caramels	35
⅓ cup	*undiluted* CARNATION Evaporated Milk	75 mL
1	pkg (175 g) semi-sweet chocolate chips	1

Place cake mix in large bowl. Cut in butter with pastry blender until mixture resembles coarse crumbs; stir in nuts. Stir in ½ cup (125 mL) evaporated milk. Spread half the batter in greased 13 x 9 x 2-inch (3.5 L) baking pan. Bake in 350°F (180°C) oven 15 min. Combine caramels and ⅓ cup (75 mL) evaporated milk in small saucepan. Cook and stir over low heat until caramels are melted. Sprinkle chocolate chips over baked layer; drizzle with hot caramel syrup; spread evenly over surface. Drop remaining batter in heaping spoonfuls over caramel mixture. Return to oven; bake 20 to 25 min. or until done. Cool completely. Cut into squares.

Makes one pan.

Parmesan Batter Bread

1 cup	boiling water	250 mL
¼ cup	butter	50 mL
¼ cup	sugar	50 mL
1½ Tbsp	dried oregano leaves, crushed	25 mL
1 tsp	salt	5 mL
1 tsp	onion salt	5 mL
½ tsp	celery salt	2 mL
1 tsp	sugar	5 mL
½ cup	lukewarm water	125 mL
2	envelopes dry granular yeast	2
1	egg, beaten	1
½ cup	grated Parmesan cheese	125 mL
3¾ to 4 cups	all purpose flour	925 to 1000 mL
⅓ cup	CARNATION Instant Skim Milk Powder	75 mL
2 Tbsp	butter, melted	30 mL
2 Tbsp	grated Parmesan cheese	30 mL

Combine boiling water, ¼ cup (50 mL) butter, ¼ cup (50 mL) sugar, oregano, salt, onion salt and celery salt; set aside. Dissolve 1 tsp (5 mL) sugar in lukewarm water in large bowl. Stir in yeast; let stand 10 min.; stir well. Stir in water-butter mixture, egg and ½ cup (125 mL) Parmesan cheese. Stir in 3 cups (750 mL) of the flour and skim milk powder. Beat until smooth and elastic. Gradually work in sufficient additional flour to make soft dough (¾ to 1 cup/175 to 250 mL more). Turn dough into large buttered bowl. Cover; let rise in warm place until double in bulk, about 1¼ hours. Stir down batter; beat vigorously ½ min. Turn into 2 greased 1-quart (1 L) casseroles. Cover; let rise in warm place until double in bulk, about ½ hour. Brush tops of loaves with 2 Tbsp (30 mL) melted butter and sprinkle with 2 Tbsp (30 mL) Parmesan cheese. Bake in 350°F (180°C) oven 40 to 45 min. or until done. Remove from pans at once and cool on wire racks.

Makes 2 loaves.

BAKING

Zucchini Spice Bread

4 cups	all purpose flour	1000 mL
2 tsp	ground cinnamon	10 mL
1½ tsp	baking powder	7 mL
1 tsp	baking soda	5 mL
1 tsp	salt	5 mL
3	eggs	3
2 cups	sugar	500 mL
1½ cups	shredded unpeeled zucchini	375 mL
¾ cup	*undiluted* CARNATION Evaporated Milk	175 mL
⅔ cup	water	150 mL
¼ cup	vegetable oil	50 mL
2 tsp	vanilla	10 mL
½ cup	chopped nuts	125 mL
	Honey Butter	

Stir together flour, cinnamon, baking powder, baking soda and salt in large bowl. Beat eggs in medium bowl; blend in sugar, zucchini, evaporated milk, water, oil and vanilla. Add to dry ingredients all at once; stir just until moistened. Stir in nuts. Turn batter into 2 greased 9 x 5 x 3-inch (1.5 L) loaf pans. Bake in 350°F (180°C) oven 55 to 60 min. or until done. Cool in pans 10 min.; remove from pans; cool completely. Slice and serve with Honey Butter.

Makes 2 loaves.

Honey Butter: Cream ½ cup (125 mL) softened butter. Beat in ⅓ cup (75 mL) honey.

Makes about 1 cup (250 mL).

BAKING

Nutty Date Squares

½ cup	butter, softened	125 mL
¼ cup	icing sugar	50 mL
1 cup	all purpose flour	250 mL
1	egg	1
¼ cup	granulated sugar	50 mL
1	pkg (92 g) vanilla pudding and pie filling	1
½ tsp	baking powder	2 mL
½ cup	*undiluted* CARNATION Evaporated Milk	125 mL
1⅔ cups	flaked coconut	400 mL
½ cup	chopped dates	125 mL
½ cup	chopped nuts	125 mL

Cream butter and icing sugar in large mixer bowl until light and fluffy. Gradually add flour. Beat 2 min. at medium speed. Press evenly onto bottom of greased 8-inch (2 L) square baking pan. Bake in 350°F (180°C) oven 15 min. Beat egg; gradually beat in granulated sugar. Stir in pudding mix, baking powder, evaporated milk, coconut, dates and nuts. Spread over hot crust. Bake 30 to 35 min. longer or until done. Cool completely. Cut into squares.

Makes one pan.

Harvest Gingerbread Cake

½ cup	*undiluted* CARNATION 2% Evaporated Milk	125 mL
2 tsp	vinegar	10 mL
2	eggs	2
½ cup	packed brown sugar	125 mL
½ cup	molasses	125 mL
½ cup	vegetable oil	125 mL
2 cups	all purpose flour	500 mL
1½ tsp	ground ginger	7 mL
1 tsp	ground cinnamon	5 mL
1 tsp	unsweetened cocoa powder	5 mL
1 tsp	baking powder	5 mL
½ tsp	salt	2 mL
¼ tsp	baking soda	1 mL
1 cup	chopped pared apple	250 mL
	Creamy Lemon Sauce	

Combine evaporated milk and vinegar; set aside. Beat eggs in large mixer bowl; beat in sugar. Stir in molasses and oil. Stir together flour, ginger, cinnamon, cocoa, baking powder, salt and baking soda in medium bowl. Add dry ingredients to egg mixture alternately with evaporated milk mixture, combining lightly after each addition. Stir in apple. Pour batter into greased 8-inch (2 L) baking pan. Bake in 325°F (160°C) oven 45 to 50 min. or until done. Serve warm with Creamy Lemon Sauce.

Makes one cake.

Creamy Lemon Sauce: Combine ½ cup (125 mL) sugar and 1 Tbsp (15 mL) corn starch in small saucepan. Stir in ½ cup (125 mL) water. Cook and stir over medium heat until mixture comes to a boil and thickens. Reduce heat; cook 1 min. longer. Add 1 Tbsp (15 mL) butter. In the following order, very slowly stir in ½ cup (125 mL) *undiluted* CARNATION 2% Evaporated Milk, ¼ cup (50 mL) lemon juice and 1½ tsp (7 mL) lemon rind. Serve warm.

Makes about 1½ cups (375 mL).

Sweet, simple and sensational...

Desserts

"We all have a major character weakness. Mine is DESSERTS! How can anyone resist? If you think you can, look through the next few pages. If the pictures don't get you, the ingredients will for sure. Good luck!"

MARGARET LANGRICK

Margaret Langrick is one of Canada's youngest acting sensations. She is best known for her "Genie" winning role (best Canadian actress) in the feature film "My American Cousin," which received favourable reviews in Canada and the United States. Miss Langrick has appeared in a number of ABC, Disney and CBC television productions.

Peach Melba *Mold*

2	pkgs (85 g *each*) peach jelly powder	2
1½ cups	boiling water	375 mL
2 cups	puréed fresh ripe peaches*	500 mL
⅔ cup	*undiluted* CARNATION 2% Evaporated Milk	150 mL
	Fresh raspberries and mint leaves	
	Raspberry Sauce	

Dissolve jelly powders in boiling water in large mixer bowl. Stir in peach purée. Chill until mixture is almost set. Beat at high speed until frothy. Gradually beat in evaporated milk; continue beating until mixture is light and airy. Pour into 6-cup (1.5 L) mold. Chill until set. Unmold. Garnish with raspberries and mint leaves. Serve with Raspberry Sauce.

Makes 6 to 8 servings.

Raspberry Sauce: Purée one pkg (425 g) frozen sweetened raspberries, thawed; strain to remove seeds. Combine 1 Tbsp (15 mL) sugar and 2 tsp (10 mL) corn starch in saucepan; stir in raspberry purée. Cook and stir over medium heat until mixture comes to a boil and thickens; reduce heat; cook 1 min. longer. Cool; chill.

Makes about 1⅔ cups (400 mL).

*Or use one can (28 ozs/796 mL) peaches, drained and puréed.

Peaches 'n' Cream Trifle

½ cup	sugar	125 mL
2 Tbsp	corn starch	30 mL
1½ cups	*undiluted* CARNATION Evaporated Milk	375 mL
1¼ cups	water	300 mL
2	eggs, beaten	2
1 tsp	vanilla	5 mL
½ tsp	almond extract	2 mL
1	pkg (298 g) frozen pound cake, thawed	1
	Peach jam	
¼ cup	orange juice	50 mL
1½ cups	fresh *or* canned sliced peaches	375 mL
	Sweetened whipped cream	
	Sliced almonds	
	Peach slices	

Combine sugar and corn starch in medium saucepan. Stir in evaporated milk and water. Cook and stir over medium heat until mixture comes to a boil and thickens; reduce heat; cook 1 min. longer. Beat small amount of hot mixture into eggs. Stir egg mixture back into saucepan. Cook and stir until sauce thickens. Remove from heat. Add vanilla and almond extract. Cover surface with plastic wrap. Cool; chill. Cut cake into 12 slices. Spread peach jam over 6 slices; top with remaining slices; cut into cubes. Place half the cubes in bottom of 2-quart (2 L) glass bowl. Sprinkle cake cubes with half the orange juice. Top with half the peach slices and half the custard sauce. Repeat layers ending with sauce. Cover; chill at least 2 hours or overnight. To serve, garnish with whipped cream, almonds and more peach slices.

Makes 6 to 8 servings.

Pink Angel Dessert

2	envelopes unflavoured gelatin	2
1 cup	water	250 mL
½ cup	sugar	125 mL
¾ cup	frozen pink lemonade concentrate	175 mL
1 cup	*undiluted* CARNATION Evaporated Milk, chilled	250 mL
	Red food colour (optional)	
3 cups	angel *or* pound cake cubes	750 mL
	Fresh fruit	

Sprinkle gelatin over water in small saucepan. Let stand 10 min. to soften. Stir in sugar. Cook and stir over low heat until gelatin is dissolved. Add frozen lemonade concentrate; chill until mixture is consistency of unbeaten egg whites. Pour into large mixer bowl. Slowly beat in evaporated milk and red food colour, if desired. Continue beating at high speed until mixture is light and fluffy, about 2 min. Fold in cake cubes. Spoon into 8½ x 4½ x 2½-inch (1.25 L) loaf pan. Chill until set. Unmold; garnish with fresh fruit.

Makes 6 to 8 servings.

Steamed Holiday Fruit Puddings

½ cup	butter, softened	125 mL
½ cup	molasses	125 mL
1	egg	1
2 cups	vanilla wafer crumbs	500 mL
1 tsp	salt	5 mL
½ tsp	baking soda	2 mL
1 tsp	ground cinnamon	5 mL
1 tsp	ground nutmeg	5 mL
¾ cup	seedless raisins	175 mL
½ cup	currants	125 mL
½ cup	chopped candied citron	125 mL
1 cup	*undiluted* CARNATION Evaporated Milk	250 mL
	Buttery Lemon Sauce	

Cream together butter, molasses and egg in large mixer bowl. Combine wafer crumbs, salt, baking soda, cinnamon and nutmeg. Stir in raisins, currants and citron. Add dry ingredients to creamed mixture alternately with evaporated milk. Fill 8 buttered 6-oz (175 mL) molds or custard cups three-quarters full; cover with foil. Pour water into electric frypan to a depth of 1 inch (2.5 cm); bring water to boil. Place molds in pan; cover and cook at 250°F (120°C) 35 to 40 min. or until done. Unmold; serve with Buttery Lemon Sauce.

Makes 8 servings.

Buttery Lemon Sauce: Combine ½ cup (125 mL) sugar and 1 Tbsp (15 mL) corn starch in small saucepan. Blend in ½ cup (125 mL) water. Cook and stir over medium heat until mixture comes to a boil and thickens; reduce heat; cook 1 min. longer. Add 1 Tbsp (15 mL) butter. In the following order, very slowly stir in ½ cup (125 mL) *undiluted* CARNATION Evaporated Milk, ¼ cup (50 mL) lemon juice and 1½ tsp (7 mL) grated lemon rind.

Makes about 1½ cups (375 mL).

D E S S E R T S

Country Kitchen Bread Pudding

10	slices raisin bread	10
¼ cup	butter, melted	50 mL
4	eggs, beaten	4
1	can (385 mL) CARNATION 2% Evaporated Milk	1
⅓ cup	water	75 mL
½ cup	sugar	125 mL
1 tsp	vanilla	5 mL
½ tsp	ground cinnamon	2 mL
½ tsp	ground nutmeg	2 mL
	Sweetened whipped cream *or* ice cream	

Cut each slice of bread into 4 pieces. Drizzle butter over bread and toss lightly. Arrange bread in greased 1½-quart (1.5 L) round baking dish. Combine eggs, evaporated milk, water, sugar, vanilla, cinnamon and nutmeg. Pour over bread. Press bread down into egg-milk mixture. Set baking dish in pan of hot water. Bake in 350°F (180°C) oven 60 min. or until knife inserted near centre comes out clean. Cool slightly. Serve with whipped cream or ice cream.

Makes 6 to 8 servings.

Christmas Cranberry Dessert

1	pkg (285 g) miniature raspberry jelly rolls*	1
2	pkgs (85 g *each*) raspberry jelly powder	2
⅔ cup	sugar	150 mL
2 cups	boiling water	500 mL
1 cup	finely-chopped fresh cranberries	250 mL
⅔ cup	CARNATION Instant Skim Milk Powder	150 mL
⅔ cup	ice water	150 mL
2 Tbsp	orange juice	30 mL

Cut jelly rolls into ¼-inch (6 mm) slices. Cover bottom of 9-inch (23 cm) springform pan with some of the slices; stand remaining slices around edge of pan. Dissolve jelly powders and sugar in boiling water in large bowl. Stir in cranberries. Chill until mixture mounds from a spoon. Meanwhile, combine skim milk powder and ice water in small mixer bowl. Beat at high speed until stiff peaks form (3 - 4 min). Add orange juice. Continue beating until stiff peaks form (3 - 4 min. longer). Fold whipped skim milk into cranberry mixture. Pour into prepared pan. Chill until set. Garnish.

Makes 6 to 8 servings.

*Or use 1 pkg (298 g) frozen pound cake, thawed and cut into ¼-inch (6 mm) slices.

Pineapple Cream Refrigerator Dessert

1⅓ cups	graham wafer crumbs	400 mL
¾ cup	sugar, divided	175 mL
¼ cup	butter, melted	50 mL
1	pkg (250 g) cream cheese, softened	1
1	can (385 mL) CARNATION Evaporated Milk	1
2	pkgs (85 g *each*) lemon jelly powder	2
1½ cups	boiling water	375 mL
1	can (19 ozs/540 mL) crushed pineapple, undrained	1

Combine wafer crumbs, ¼ cup (50 mL) of the sugar and butter. Press onto bottom and side of 9-inch (23 cm) springform pan or 13 x 9 x 2-inch (3.5 L) baking dish. Bake in 375°F (190°C) oven 8 min. Cool. Beat cream cheese and remaining ½ cup (125 mL) sugar until light and smooth. Gradually beat in evaporated milk. Dissolve jelly powders in boiling water. Slowly add to evaporated milk mixture. Add undrained pineapple; blend well. Pour into prepared pan. Chill until firm. Cut into squares to serve.

Makes one pan.

DESSERTS

Chocolate Ripple Cheesecake Squares

1 cup	graham wafer crumbs	250 mL
3 Tbsp	sugar	45 mL
¼ cup	butter, melted	50 mL
1	pkg (250 g) cream cheese, softened	1
¾ cup	*undiluted* CARNATION Evaporated Milk	175 mL
½ cup	sugar	125 mL
1	egg	1
2 Tbsp	flour	30 mL
2 tsp	vanilla	10 mL
½ cup	semi-sweet chocolate chips	125 mL

Combine wafer crumbs, 3 Tbsp (45 mL) sugar and butter. Press onto bottom of 8-inch (2 L) square cake pan. Place cream cheese, evaporated milk, ½ cup (125 mL) sugar, egg, flour and vanilla in blender container; cover and blend until smooth. In small saucepan melt chocolate chips over low heat. Gradually stir ½ cup (125 mL) of the cream cheese mixture into melted chocolate. Drizzle half the chocolate mixture over crumb crust. Pour vanilla mixture over all. Drizzle remaining chocolate mixture over top. Draw a knife through batter to swirl. Bake in 300°F (150°C) oven 40 to 45 min. or until set. Cool; chill. Cut into squares to serve.

Makes one pan.

Super Chocolate Ice Cream

4	squares (28 g *each*) unsweetened chocolate	4
1 cup	sugar	250 mL
2	cans (385 mL *each*) CARNATION Evaporated Milk, divided	2
1 Tbsp	vanilla	15 mL

Mix chocolate, sugar and 1 cup (250 mL) of the evaporated milk in medium saucepan. Cook and stir until chocolate is melted. Beat with rotary beater until mixture is smooth. Add remaining evaporated milk and vanilla. Beat again until smooth. Chill. Pour into freezer container. Cover and freeze according to manufacturer's directions.

Makes about 1 quart (1 L).

Special Strawberry Ice Cream

1	pkg (425 g) frozen sweetened sliced strawberries, thawed	1
1	can (385 mL) CARNATION Evaporated Milk	1
6 Tbsp	sugar	90 mL
1 Tbsp	lemon juice	15 mL
1½ tsp	vanilla	7 mL
	Pinch salt	

Crush strawberries in their syrup. Add evaporated milk, sugar, lemon juice, vanilla and salt. Stir until well blended. Chill. Pour into freezer container. Cover and freeze according to manufacturer's directions.

Makes about 1 quart (1 L).

D E S S E R T S

Light-as-a-Cloud Citrus Pudding

1 cup	*undiluted* CARNATION 2% Evaporated Milk	250 mL
⅔ cup	sugar	150 mL
3 Tbsp	flour	45 mL
¼ tsp	salt	1 mL
2 tsp	grated lemon rind*	10 mL
¼ cup	lemon juice*	50 mL
2	eggs, separated	2
2 Tbsp	sugar	30 mL
	Icing sugar	

Place evaporated milk, ⅔ cup (150 mL) sugar, flour, salt and lemon rind in blender container. Cover and blend 20 sec. or until smooth. Add lemon juice and egg yolks. Blend at high speed 10 sec. or until well combined. Beat egg whites until frothy. Gradually beat in 2 Tbsp (30 mL) sugar until stiff peaks form. Fold blended mixture into beaten egg whites. Pour into 1-quart (1 L) casserole. Set in pan of hot water. Bake in 350°F (180°C) oven 50 to 60 min. or until done. Dust top with icing sugar. Garnish.

Makes 4 to 6 servings.

*Orange rind and juice, lime rind and juice or a combination of lemon and lime rinds and juices may be substituted.

Pecan Sauced Custard

1	can (385 mL) CARNATION Evaporated Milk	1
1 cup	water	250 mL
⅔ cup	granulated sugar	150 mL
1½ tsp	vanilla	7 mL
¼ tsp	salt	1 mL
5	eggs	5
⅓ cup	packed brown sugar	75 mL
⅓ cup	chopped pecans	75 mL
¼ tsp	ground cinnamon	1 mL
	Pinch ground nutmeg	

Combine evaporated milk and water in saucepan; scald. Add granulated sugar, vanilla and salt. Stir until sugar is dissolved. Beat eggs well. Gradually stir in hot milk mixture. Pour into 5-cup (1.25 L) shallow baking dish.* Place in pan of hot water. Bake in 300°F (150°C) oven about 40 min. or until knife inserted near centre comes out clean. Combine brown sugar, nuts, cinnamon and nutmeg. Sprinkle over top of custard. Cover with plastic wrap immediately. Cool; chill until sugar liquifies.

Makes 6 servings.

*Or six 6-oz (175 mL) custard cups. Bake 30 to 35 min.

DESSERTS

Five Minute Fudge

1⅔ cups	sugar	400 mL
⅔ cup	*undiluted* CARNATION Evaporated Milk	150 mL
2 Tbsp	butter	30 mL
½ tsp	salt	2 mL
2 cups	miniature marshmallows	500 mL
1½ cups	semi-sweet chocolate chips	375 mL
1 tsp	vanilla	5 mL
½ cup	chopped walnuts	125 mL

Combine sugar, evaporated milk, butter and salt in medium saucepan. Bring to full boil over medium heat; stir constantly. Boil 4 to 5 min.; stir constantly. Remove from heat. Stir in marshmallows, chocolate chips, vanilla and nuts. Stir vigorously 1 min. until marshmallows melt and blend. Pour into buttered 8-inch (2 L) square cake pan. Chill. Cut into squares. Store in refrigerator.

Peanut Butter Fudge: Substitute peanut butter chips for chocolate chips and chopped peanuts for walnuts. Melt 1 cup (250 mL) semi-sweet chocolate chips in small saucepan over low heat. Spread on fudge.

Makes about 2 pounds (1 kg).

DESSERTS

Deliciously Decadent Truffles

½ cup	*undiluted* CARNATION Evaporated Milk	125 mL
¼ cup	sugar	50 mL
1	pkg (350 g) semi-sweet chocolate chips	1
2 Tbsp	rum *or* liqueur*	30 mL
	CARNATION Hot Chocolate Mix	
	Icing sugar	
	Finely-chopped toasted coconut	
	Finely-chopped toasted nuts	

Combine evaporated milk and sugar in small saucepan. Cook and stir over medium heat until mixture comes to a full rolling boil. Boil 3 min.; stir constantly. Remove from heat. Add chocolate chips and rum; stir until chocolate melts. Chill until cool enough to handle. Shape into 1-inch (2.5 cm) balls. Roll in hot chocolate mix, icing sugar, coconut or nuts. Cover and store at room temperature.

Makes about 2½ dozen candies.

*Use coffee, chocolate, orange, mint or your favourite liqueur.

Chocolate Fudge Sauce

4	squares (28 g *each*) semi-sweet chocolate	4
1 cup	*undiluted* CARNATION Evaporated Milk	250 mL
¼ cup	sugar	50 mL
	Pinch salt	
1 tsp	vanilla	5 mL

Place chocolate squares in 1-quart (1 L) glass measure. Microwave, uncovered, at HIGH (100%) 2 min. or until melted; stir well. Gradually stir in evaporated milk, sugar and salt. Microwave, covered, at HIGH (100%) 2 min. or until mixture boils and thickens; stir twice while cooking. Add vanilla.

Makes about 1 cup (250 mL).

Chocolate Peanut Butter Sauce: Stir ¼ cup (50 mL) smooth peanut butter into melted chocolate before adding remaining ingredients.

Makes about 1¼ cups (300 mL).

Butterscotch Sauce

2 cups	packed brown sugar	500 mL
1 cup	*undiluted* CARNATION Evaporated Milk	250 mL
3 Tbsp	corn syrup	45 mL
⅓ cup	butter	75 mL
1 tsp	vanilla	5 mL

Combine sugar, evaporated milk and corn syrup in 1-quart (1 L) glass measure. Add butter. Microwave, uncovered, at HIGH (100%) 1 min.; stir. Reduce power to MEDIUM (50%); microwave, uncovered, 1½ to 2 min. longer or until heated through; stir once while cooking. (Do not boil.) Add vanilla.

Makes about 2½ cups (625 mL).

DESSERTS

Fancy these...

Pies & Tarts

"If you're a true fancier of the finer things in life, if you recognize greatness when you see it, feel it or taste it, then welcome to the world of pies and tarts. It's my world and I love every delectable moment. You're invited too! Turn the page to begin."

ANDY DONATO

Andy Donato is recognized as one of Canada's most prolific editorial cartoonists. He joined the Toronto Sun as art director and in 1974 began cartooning on a full-time basis. In 1980, he won "Best editorial cartoon in the world" from the Montreal Salon of Cartoons. In 1985 Mr. Donato was elected president of the Association of American Editorial Cartoonists.

Strawberry Cheesecake Pie

1½ cups	vanilla wafer crumbs	375 mL
¼ cup	butter, melted	50 mL
1	pkg (250 g) cream cheese, softened	1
½ cup	sugar	125 mL
2 Tbsp	flour	30 mL
1	egg	1
⅔ cup	*undiluted* CARNATION 2% Evaporated Milk	150 mL
1 tsp	grated lemon rind	5 mL
¼ cup	lemon juice	50 mL
2 cups	hulled fresh strawberries	500 mL
½ cup	strawberry *or* red currant jelly	125 mL

Combine wafer crumbs and butter; press onto bottom and side of 9-inch (23 cm) pie plate; set aside. Beat cream cheese until light in small mixer bowl. Beat in sugar, flour and egg. Gradually beat in evaporated milk. Add lemon rind and juice; stir to blend. Pour into prepared crust. Bake in 325°F (160°C) oven 30 to 35 min. Cool completely. Halve strawberries; arrange on top of pie. Melt strawberry jelly in small saucepan. Carefully spoon over berries. Chill well before serving.

To Microwave: Place butter in 9-inch (23 cm) glass pie plate. Microwave, uncovered, at HIGH (100%) 45 sec. or until butter melts. Add wafer crumbs; stir with fork to combine. Press onto bottom and side of pie plate. Prepare filling as above. Pour into prepared crust. Microwave, uncovered, at MEDIUM LOW (30%) 13 to 15 min. or until set in centre; give pie quarter turn three times while cooking. Cool completely. Prepare fruit topping as above.

Makes one pie.

Apple Crisp Pie

3 cups	pared sliced apples	750 mL
3 cups	water, divided	750 mL
1 cup	CARNATION Instant Skim Milk Powder	250 mL
⅔ cup	granulated sugar	150 mL
⅓ cup	corn starch	75 mL
½ tsp	salt	2 mL
2	eggs, beaten	2
1 tsp	vanilla	5 mL
⅓ cup	packed brown sugar	75 mL
¼ cup	all purpose flour	50 mL
¼ cup	quick cooking rolled oats	50 mL
½ tsp	ground cinnamon	2 mL
¼ tsp	ground nutmeg	1 mL
3 Tbsp	butter	45 mL
1	(9-inch/23 cm) baked pastry shell	1

Cook apple slices in ½ cup (125 mL) of the water in covered saucepan 10 min. or until tender; drain. Combine skim milk powder, granulated sugar, corn starch and salt in medium saucepan. Stir in remaining 2½ cups (625 mL) water. Cook and stir over medium heat, until mixture comes to a boil and thickens. Reduce heat; cook 1 min. longer. Beat small amount of hot mixture into eggs; stir egg mixture back into saucepan. Cook and stir until mixture thickens. Remove from heat. Add vanilla. Cover surface with plastic wrap; cool custard slightly. Combine brown sugar, flour, oats, cinnamon and nutmeg in small bowl; cut in butter with pastry blender until mixture resembles coarse crumbs. Place apple slices on bottom of pastry shell. Pour custard over apples. Sprinkle brown sugar mixture over top. Bake in 375°F (190°C) oven 15 min. Cool; chill.

Makes one pie.

Frosty Blueberry Pie

1 cup	graham wafer crumbs	250 mL
2 Tbsp	sugar	30 mL
¼ cup	butter, melted	50 mL
38 to 40	(about ½ lb/250 g) marshmallows	38 to 40
1 cup	*undiluted* CARNATION Evaporated Milk, divided	250 mL
1 Tbsp	lemon juice	15 mL
1 cup	fresh *or* frozen blueberries, thawed*	250 mL
1 Tbsp	grated lemon rind	15 mL

Combine wafer crumbs, sugar and butter. Press onto bottom and side of 9-inch (23 cm) pie plate. Bake in 325°F (160°C) oven 7 to 8 min. Cool. Combine marshmallows and ½ cup (125 mL) of the evaporated milk in saucepan; cook and stir over medium heat until syrupy. Chill remaining ½ cup (125 mL) evaporated milk in metal cake pan in freezer until soft ice crystals form around edges of pan (10 - 15 min.). Whip until stiff (2 min.). Add lemon juice. Whip very stiff (2 min. longer). Fold whipped evaporated milk, blueberries and lemon rind into cooled marshmallow mixture. Spoon into prepared pie shell. Freeze until firm. Wrap to store. Remove to refrigerator ½ hour before cutting and serving.

Makes one pie.

*If berries are large, chop coarsely.

Carnation
Classic Pumpkin Pie

2	eggs, beaten	2
1½ cups	canned pumpkin	375 mL
1 cup	sugar	250 mL
½ tsp	salt	2 mL
1 tsp	ground cinnamon	5 mL
¼ tsp	ground ginger	1 mL
¼ tsp	ground cloves	1 mL
¼ tsp	ground nutmeg	1 mL
1½ cups	*undiluted* CARNATION Evaporated Milk	375 mL
1	(9-inch/23 cm) unbaked pastry shell	1
	Baked pastry cut-outs	

Combine eggs, pumpkin, sugar, salt, cinnamon, ginger, cloves and nutmeg in large bowl. Gradually stir in evaporated milk; mix well. Pour into pastry shell. Bake in 350°F (180°C) oven 50 to 55 min. or until knife inserted near centre comes out clean. Cool completely. Garnish with pastry cut-outs.

Praline Topped Pumpkin Pie: Combine ½ cup (125 mL) chopped pecans, ⅓ cup (75 mL) packed brown sugar and 3 Tbsp (45 mL) melted butter. Sprinkle over pie after 30 min. baking time. Continue baking 20 to 25 min.

Makes one pie.

Banana Chocolate Cream Pie

1 cup	sugar, divided	225 mL
⅓ cup	corn starch	75 mL
½ tsp	salt	2 mL
1	can (385 mL) CARNATION Evaporated Milk	1
1 cup	water	250 mL
3	eggs, separated	3
3	squares (28 g *each*) semi-sweet chocolate, melted	3
1 tsp	vanilla	5 mL
1	large ripe banana, sliced	1
1	(9-inch/23 cm) baked pastry shell	1

Combine ⅔ cup (150 mL) of the sugar, corn starch and salt in medium saucepan. Stir in evaporated milk and water. Cook and stir over medium heat until mixture comes to a boil and thickens; reduce heat; cook 1 min. longer. Remove from heat. Beat egg yolks slightly. Beat small amount of hot mixture into egg yolks. Stir egg mixture back into saucepan. Cook and stir until mixture thickens. Remove from heat. Add chocolate and vanilla. Arrange banana slices in bottom of pastry shell. Pour hot pudding evenly over banana. Beat egg whites until frothy. Gradually beat in remaining ⅓ cup (75 mL) sugar until stiff peaks form. Bake in 400°F (200°C) oven 8 to 10 min. or until lightly browned. Cool.

To Microwave: Combine ⅔ cup (150 mL) of the sugar, corn starch and salt in 2-quart (2 L) glass measure. Gradually stir in evaporated milk and water. Microwave, uncovered, at HIGH (100%) 6½ to 7½ min. or until mixture boils and thickens; stir 2 or 3 times while cooking. Beat egg yolks slightly. Stir some of hot mixture into egg yolks; stir egg mixture back into measure. Microwave, uncovered, at HIGH (100%) 1 min. Add chocolate and vanilla; stir until melted. Complete as above.

Makes one pie.

Tarte au Sucre

2 cups	packed brown sugar	500 mL
3 Tbsp	flour	45 mL
1	can (385 mL) CARNATION Evaporated Milk	1
2	eggs, beaten	2
1 tsp	vanilla	5 mL
½ cup	chopped pecans (optional)	125 mL
1	(9-inch/23 cm) unbaked pastry shell	1
	Baked pastry cut-outs	

Combine brown sugar and flour. Blend in evaporated milk, eggs and vanilla. Stir in nuts. Pour into pastry shell. Bake in 375°F (190°C) oven 35 to 40 min. or until puffed and brown. Cool completely. Garnish with pastry cut-outs.

Makes one pie.

Fresh Fruit
Chiffon Tarts

¾ cup	sugar, divided	175 mL
¼ cup	corn starch	50 mL
¾ cup	*undiluted* CARNATION 2% Evaporated Milk	175 mL
½ cup	water	125 mL
2	eggs, separated	2
1 tsp	grated lemon rind	5 mL
3 Tbsp	lemon juice	45 mL
24	(2 to 3-inch/5 to 7 cm) baked cooled tart shells	24
	Fresh raspberries or any fresh fruit	

Combine ½ cup (125 mL) of the sugar and corn starch in small saucepan. Stir in evaporated milk and water. Cook and stir over medium heat until mixture comes to a boil and thickens; reduce heat; cook 1 min. longer. Remove from heat. Beat egg yolks slightly. Beat small amount of hot mixture into egg yolks. Stir egg mixture back into saucepan. Cook and stir until mixture thickens. Remove from heat. Add lemon rind and juice. Cover surface with plastic wrap. Cool; chill. Beat egg whites until frothy. Gradually beat in remaining ¼ cup (50 mL) sugar until stiff peaks form. Beat chilled lemon mixture until smooth; fold in beaten egg whites. Spoon into prepared tart shells; top with fresh raspberries. Garnish.

Makes 24 tarts.

Notes

Recipe Ingredient Savings

30¢   30¢

SAVE
30¢

**when you purchase
2 cans of**

Carnation®

30¢   **Evaporated Milk 385 mL (Regular or 2%)**

TO DEALER:
This coupon will be redeemed for 30¢, plus our specified handling fee provided it has been used solely toward the purchase of 2 cans of Carnation Evaporated Milk 385 mL (Regular or 2%). Any other application constitutes fraud. Invoices proving purchase of sufficient Carnation Evaporated Milk (Regular or 2%) (in the previous 90 days) to cover coupons presented for redemption must be shown upon request. Offer void where taxed, prohibited or otherwise restricted by law. This coupon is issued by Carnation. We reserve the right to refuse to honour redemption through outside agencies, brokers etc. Unauthorized reproduction of this coupon is prohibited. For redemption, mail to: Carnation, P.O. Box 3000, Saint John, New Brunswick E2L 4L3, OFFER GOOD ONLY IN CANADA, LIMIT ONE COUPON PER PURCHASE. NO EXPIRY DATE.

4731455H

30¢   30¢

SAVE
30¢

**when you purchase
2 cans of**

Carnation®

30¢   **Evaporated Milk 385 mL (Regular or 2%)**

TO DEALER:
This coupon will be redeemed for 30¢, plus our specified handling fee provided it has been used solely toward the purchase of 2 cans of Carnation Evaporated Milk 385 mL (Regular or 2%). Any other application constitutes fraud. Invoices proving purchase of sufficient Carnation Evaporated Milk (Regular or 2%) (in the previous 90 days) to cover coupons presented for redemption must be shown upon request. Offer void where taxed, prohibited or otherwise restricted by law. This coupon is issued by Carnation. We reserve the right to refuse to honour redemption through outside agencies, brokers etc. Unauthorized reproduction of this coupon is prohibited. For redemption, mail to: Carnation, P.O. Box 3000, Saint John, New Brunswick E2L 4L3, OFFER GOOD ONLY IN CANADA, LIMIT ONE COUPON PER PURCHASE. NO EXPIRY DATE.

4731455H

75¢   75¢

75¢
OFF

500 g or 1 kg size

Carnation®
Instant Skim Milk Powder

TO DEALER:
This coupon will be redeemed for 75¢, plus our specified handling fee provided it has been used solely toward the purchase of Carnation Instant Skim Milk Powder 500 g or 1 kg. Any other application constitutes fraud. Invoices proving purchase of sufficient Carnation Instant Skim Milk Powder (in the previous 90 days) to cover coupons presented for redemption must be shown upon request. Offer void where taxed, prohibited or otherwise restricted by law. This coupon is issued by Carnation. We reserve the right to refuse to honour redemption through outside agencies, brokers etc. Unauthorized reproduction of this coupon is prohibited. For redemption, mail to: Carnation, P.O. Box 3000, Saint John, New Brunswick E2L 4L3, OFFER GOOD ONLY IN CANADA, LIMIT ONE COUPON PER PURCHASE. NO EXPIRY DATE.

75¢   **"Great for Recipes and an Excellent Source of Calcium"**

4731466H

Économisez sur ces ingrédients de recettes

Recipe Ingredient Savings

Économisez sur ces ingrédients de recettes

YOU CAN HELP EVEN MORE!

Canadian Best Seller!

Celebrity Classics

Recipe classics collected from the Carnation Kitchens

All profits from the sale of this book will be donated to the Multiple Sclerosis Society of Canada. **MS**

ORDER ADDITIONAL COPIES OF Celebrity Classics

- The ideal gift for family members or friends
- Over 100 mouthwatering recipe classics to choose from
- All profits will support the Multiple Sclerosis Society of Canada

If you do not wish to order at this time please pass this form along to a friend. If form is detached send your name and address along with $12.95 cheque (or money order) payable to the Multiple Sclerosis Society of Canada for each book ordered to:

Multiple Sclerosis Society of Canada
CELEBRITY CLASSICS OFFER
250 Bloor Street East, Suite 820
Toronto, Ontario M4W 3P9

TAKE NOTE OF A BEAUTIFUL WAY TO SUPPORT MS

Multiple Sclerosis Society
of Canada

SUPPORT THE CARNATION CAMPAIGN FOR MS

Multiple Sclerosis Society
of Canada

Order a set of ten 4″ × 6″ NOTE CARDS & ENVELOPES beautifully mouth painted in vibrant watercolours by Kathy Harvey who has multiple sclerosis.

PROCEEDS FROM THE SALE OF THESE CARDS WILL SUPPORT THE MULTIPLE SCLEROSIS SOCIETY OF CANADA.

If you do not wish to order at this time please pass this form along to a friend. If form is detached send your name and address along with $6.95 cheque (or money order) payable to the Multiple Sclerosis Society of Canada for each Note Card set to:

Multiple Sclerosis Society of Canada, NOTE CARD OFFER
250 Bloor Street East, Suite 820, Toronto, Ontario M4W 3P9

ORDER FORM

YES, I'd like to order NOTE CARD sets.

Enclosed is my cheque (or money order) payable to the Multiple Sclerosis Society of Canada worth

$6.95* for each set × _____ = $ _____
            INDICATE NO. OF   TOTAL
            SETS ORDERED

OR Please charge purchase to my
    ☐ VISA ☐ MASTERCARD

_____   _____
CARD NUMBER   EXPIRY DATE

SIGNATURE _____

*Price includes $5.95 for cards plus $1.00 to cover postage and handling.

NAME _____

ADDRESS _____

_____ APT. _____

CITY _____

PROV. _____   POSTAL
                        CODE _____

TELEPHONE _____

Please, allow 6 - 8 weeks for delivery.

WHEN ORDERING COOKBOOK AND/OR NOTE CARDS, PLEASE ENCLOSE THIS COMPLETED ORDER FROM IN AN ENVELOPE, ALONG WITH YOUR PAYMENT, AND MAIL TO:

Multiple Sclerosis Society of Canada, MS OFFER
250 Bloor Street East, Suite 820, Toronto, Ontario M4W 3P9